THE WINNING
Mix

Launch and grow your food business without selling your soul

Save time, money and sanity by learning from my lessons

Claire Brumby

Printed in the United Kingdom

First Printing, 2018

Print ISBN 978-1-9164249-0-6
Ebook ISBN 978-1-9164249-1-3

Claire Brumby
PO Box 130
BRIGG
DN20 2AZ

www.clairebrumby.com

Praise for The Winning Mix

I met Claire at Pitch@Palace in November 2015 and over the next few months, was able to give her some help, advice and support about Scrubbys at an important time for her. I'm always very impressed with anyone who can build a product-based brand in a very tough marketplace, and her insight, learnings and 'diamonds' within this book will for sure help others succeed. Wishing her the very best for the future, and in her epic open ocean swimming challenges too!

Will King | Founder | King of Shaves

In the Food Business? You NEED this book!

A unique take and look at Life, Business and Food.

The book I wish I'd written.

Motivational. Educational. Inspirational.

The right ingredients twinned with the perfect recipe: 10/10.

Brad Burton | The UK's #1 Motivational Business Speaker | www.bradburton.biz

Passion. Determination. Knowledge. Straight talking advice! Wow! This book has it all.

If you're in the business of food and in need of advice – or just a good, honest, well-aimed kick from someone who knows their stuff – you need this book. Stop scouring Google. Shred everything you've read before and stop wasting your time. Claire Brumby is an authority in her field and an awesome businesswoman to boot – and she's poured all her knowledge into these pages. It's like having an expert coach on tap.

Read the book. Do the exercises. Learn from the expert. This book could be the very thing to turn your life – and food business – around.

Taz Thornton | www.tazthornton.com

This book takes you on a journey and shows what you can achieve and overcome in life.

The information in this book could save you so much time and thousands of pounds if you are thinking of creating a brand in the food world.

Claire is a remarkable person and her story is only just beginning.

I highly recommend this book.

Croz Crossley (The Mindset Technician) | www.croz.uk.com

This compelling and informative book is food for thought, inspiration, and absolutely essential reading for any food or drink start-up keen to succeed.

Tessa Stuart | www.tessastuart.co.uk

Claire's zest for life, expertise and methodical and practical application of her knowledge shine through in her writing, making this an enjoyable and informed read for any budding food business.

Jane Milton | www.janemilton.com

The delight of Claire's book is that it is 'warts and all'. She has written from the heart and it flows as a vivid account of a journey to create a food business from someone who has lived and breathed the ups and downs, the twists and turns.

What makes it most interesting is that it combines a factual account of Claire's trials and tribulations in creating and developing Scrubbys whilst at the same time weaving in her many coaching messages.

The result is that it isn't just a biographical story of a businesswoman, nor is it a self-help manual for budding entrepreneurs. It is both.

Julian Wild | Partner | Rollits LLP | www.rollits.com

Over the last 14 years I have coached and mentored 100s of business owners, entrepreneurs and industry leaders. I have learnt that all the great ones have success inherent in their DNA. After spending less than an hour with Claire it was apparent she was most certainly one of these people; she was destined for success.

Claire is upbeat, positive, driven, tenacious and extremely smart. Irrespective of her chosen calling it was clear when we first met that once she focused on something she would be successful. Her first book, *The Winning Mix*, and her consultancy business The Food Guide are the perfect platforms for her to exercise these traits and skills. Paying forward her wealth of knowledge, experience, and understanding in a tough and uncompromising industry, you couldn't want for a better mentor alongside you on your own food journey.

Ian Dickson | International Speaker & Award-Winning Business Coach | www.iandickson.co.uk

I wish I had read this book before I started on my entrepreneurial journey but it has served as a real reminder that the braver you are the more successful you will be, so please note how brave Claire was and make sure you replicate her tenacity and determination to make things happen.

Lorna Davidson | CEO | The Mothership Group | www.themothershipgroup.com

This book is an essential read and business tool for anyone considering starting a food business or looking to grow and move a food business to the next level. Claire invites the reader to join her on her roller coaster journey from conception to launching and growing her food enterprise. The reader experiences and learns first-hand the highs and lows and gains a unique insight into starting and developing a food business. Claire's 'diamonds' and what she would do differently now will support the reader on their entrepreneurial food journey. Claire's honest account of the personal cost to her and her family allows the reader into her heart and soul. The passion Claire clearly invested into her own business is now transferred into supporting and mentoring food entrepreneurs to thrive and grow.

Julie Earnshaw | Privileged to have been at the birth of Scrubbys

Contents

Life or Death
— Choose Life

My life was about to change forever. It was 13th August 2005. I was at work; it was a pretty normal day. At that time, I was in the hospitality industry, managing a hotel and spa. It was a normal high-stress day, and I was flying around the hotel when suddenly I experienced crushing chest pains. I couldn't breathe or stand. I thought I was having a heart attack, although why I don't know, as I had no idea what a heart attack felt like. That's just what my brain was telling me.

I will never forget the crushing feeling. I had never felt a pain or feeling like it. Something was very wrong. I was stood near the reception desk and grabbed onto it, utterly breathless. The pain just hit me from nowhere. I hadn't felt ill. I wasn't unwell. It just came on within a second and totally floored me.

My kids were at this time one, four and seven years old. I had worked throughout each pregnancy and went straight back to work after they were all born, in fact, just days after in the case of my middle daughter as her birthday is the 15th December, one of the peaks in the hospitality industry. I was no stranger to stress or hard work, but these pains were something else.

I didn't know what to think. What on earth was happening to me? My staff sat me down, then after a minute or so the pains subsided. Everyone around me was advising that they call an ambulance, but because the pains had eased I didn't want to bother anyone so I decided to drive myself to my doctor.

After I arrived at the doctors, everything became a bit of a blur. I remember my doctor telling me that he thought it was a Pulmonary Embolism (PE – the sudden blockage of a major blood vessel in the lung by a blood clot), and he needed to get me to hospital immediately or I might die.

When I arrived at hospital, I remember the nurses trying to take blood samples: trying as it was proving very difficult to get any from my veins. They took blood from my wrist veins, but it was clotting too fast for them to get it to the lab to test it, a clear sign that PE was extremely likely. At this point I passed out, and I don't recall much of what happened during the next few days.

It turned out that the doctor was right. It wasn't a heart attack as I had suspected; I was an extremely lucky survivor of a Pulmonary Embolism (I do not know what the survival rates were back then, but I know there was a very real chance that I would die), and had it not been for the fast action by the doctors and hospital teams, I would not have survived.

I was in hospital for 10 days having scans, tests, and medication. We never told the kids just how ill I was at the time. I remember my husband, John, bringing them in to the hospital, and I would let them lie in bed with me, eating marshmallows and playing games on the hospital TV monitor. They just thought I was having a rest. I couldn't see them for more than five minutes at a time, I was so exhausted.

Now I don't want to get all 'woo-woo' on you here, but I did choose to live. I was so weak, exhausted and wasn't sure if I could carry on breathing. I remember being asked (don't ask me by who; it wasn't a person), did I want to stay or go? What? Stay or go? Are you crazy? Of course I am staying. My kids need me. I ran through all the occasions they would need me: the first bras for the girls, periods, boyfriends, getting married. And George was just 13 months old; he wouldn't even remember me. All these things and occasions flashed through my brain. Flashed in one sense, but I felt as though I was actually living them.

I felt strangely calm, safe, and totally pain-free whilst this 'conversation' was going on. There was no question about it though. I was staying; I wasn't going. My kids needed me.

I remember the song playing on the radio when I came round: Daniel Powter – 'Bad Day'. To this day when I hear that song I recall that feeling of being in my hospital bed and choosing to stay.

Claire's Diamond

Choose life... whatever you do make sure you're happy; we are not here forever.

This book is dedicated to my three amazing kids, love you all the world xxx

Hello Gorgeous Foodies

*W*hy gorgeous foodies? This is what I started calling my followers on social media, and it's kind of stuck! So, from here on in, I hope you don't mind, but you're one of my many and fabulous gorgeous foodies now!

My near-death experience was the catalyst that led to the next decision in my life: creating and launching a food business, and ultimately the reason for writing this book.

Knowing your why is important in any situation. My 'why' and 'passion' in writing this book is to help you on your entrepreneurial journey.

So now you know my why: the reason I decided to launch a food business. This brought many challenges along the way especially given I wasn't from a food background. Don't worry, I will share them throughout the book, as I feel you will find them really useful.

What's **YOUR** why?

- Have you been dreaming up a food business for years but don't know how to start?
- Would you like to hear how someone else did it?
- Do you just need a push or some encouragement?
- Are you stuck in a job you don't like?
- Do you believe you have the next big product success story?

If you've picked up this book, you're probably thinking of launching your food business or you already have and are looking for some help, guidance or even reassurance right now.

Or you could be embarking on your own entrepreneurial journey, not in the world of food, but would like to hear about a fellow entrepreneur's journey, which will, believe me, confirm to you that you are not alone in all your struggles, endeavours, sleepless nights, insane highs over the smallest of wins and the generally 'unique' way you lead your life (some would say crazy!).

In this book, I will share my story – warts and all – and what I've learnt on my journey. I don't intend to give you a 'fully comprehensive' guide, as there are many resources out there already for you to find that information in, some of which I will share with you throughout the book.

I will touch on what to do, the stages to take – broken down into 8 key steps – and why I suggest you do these, but I hope to be more of an 'inspiration' rather than an 'instruction'.

I personally think the best gift and insight I can give you is my honesty, experience and personal insights. Through these I am sure:

- You will find answers to whatever you are grappling with now.
- You will take comfort from knowing you are not alone.
- You'll find your own courage to either take your leap and not be afraid of the risks, or realise actually it's not for you to take that leap, but at least you can stop tormenting yourself; you will have made a decision.
- You'll find courage to continue if you are facing tough times right now.
- You'll have had my help to avoid being amongst the 1 in 4 entrepreneurs who fail in the first 24 months.

My experience led to me founding a food brand, Scrubbys (vegetable crisps), which my husband and I launched in 2012. Throughout this book I'm going to take you on that journey, of just why and how we did that, but also share with you what I know now (as I have learnt so much since I was that fledgling food entrepreneur) and some useful information which I am sure will help you in your business.

I am going to take you 'behind' the Scrubbys brand. I will share with you:

- How I used guerrilla marketing and the amazing wins it gave me.
- How I got a picture of Chris Evans with a bag of Scrubbys in his mouth.

- Why I found myself at St James's Palace twice as a food entrepreneur.
- How I sipped on royal champagne whilst meeting royalty.
- My *Dragons' Den* experience.
- How I've failed at times, but why this has helped mould me into who I am now.
- Some amazing top tips to save you time, money and sanity on your journey.

Every single challenger brand you see on the shelves in your local supermarket will without a doubt have a story of how/why that brand is there. Each of these brands will have a story about the founders, and there will be a story about the product: how or why it was created.

So the next time you walk past and see all of these on the shelves, know that you are looking into people's lives, and if you are in the throes of creating your own brand, be proud, work your arse off, and keep your belief that your brand will make it onto those very shelves where you too will have shoppers engaging in your life and story through your product and brand.

So, how do you use this book?

- If you just want to know what I did, you'll find that section at the front of each chapter.
- If you want the information on how to do certain steps yourself, you'll find that in the second section of each chapter, 'The Practical Stuff'. I have developed a structure and a process, and this is what I work through with my clients, an 8-stage process to launching. All the stages are covered throughout the chapters.
- Then if you want to know 'What Would Claire Do Now?' with the hindsight and knowledge I have now, you'll find that at the end of each chapter.
- There is then the opportunity for you to jot down all your ideas after reading my journey, and advice for the next steps: what YOU should do now.
- At the back of the book, you'll find a ton of really useful stuff: top tips, reference sites, and valuable 'bites' of information.

`Claire's Diamonds`

Throughout the book, to help you and give some added encouragement, or insights, however you want to view them, you'll see these. They'll be randomly scattered throughout, and I believe will give you some 'oomph' relevant to where you may be in line with what I was feeling and facing at a particular juncture in my journey.

These are 'digestible snippets' so if you choose to just dip in and out of this book, you will have something of value each time you pick it up, flick through it and put it down. Look out for them! Clearly, I hope you read the entire book – but if you're anything like me you may dip in and out!

You will also find 'Real Accounts', which are some case studies of businesses I have helped in these past few years through my consultancy, mentoring and coaching services which I now offer.

Now, at this stage I should warn you that there is some swearing throughout this book, but whilst you'll find the odd swearword, at the points when you read these, you'll have full understanding as to why they're there; I am being very honest, and in the few places where these words appear, they are an absolute true reflection of the pain, stress or feeling being experienced at that time.

CHAPTER 1

Leaping into the Unknown

ALL OR NOTHING, IT'S THE ONLY WAY TO BE. TRUST ME, THE NET OR WAY WILL ONLY APPEAR AFTER THE LEAP.

My pulmonary embolism (PE) knocked me for six. It also affected John, my husband, and our kids, not to mention that I couldn't work, nor could John as he had to look after them. I had no upper body strength for months, and I felt (and looked) deathly ill for a long time.

The fatigue was overwhelming on most days for a good number of months, with the simplest of things like walking up the stairs or showering and getting dressed seeming impossible.

I was having weekly blood tests (INR – international normalised ratio) which measure how long it takes for your blood to clot, thereby indicating the dose of blood thinning medication required. The tests went on for months, and I was also having tablets and injections daily, but my body didn't like the medication, and expressed this with severe joint pains and hair loss.

Now, there was no way I was settling for that. I was exhausted to my bones, looked like death, was helpless at times to look after my kids, but there was no way I was living with this pain and losing my hair too.

It was a confusing and extremely stressful time for us as we weren't sure just how long my recovery would take. When would I be well enough to work again? I would ask the doctors, but they couldn't say for definite. Every person who experiences a PE has an individual recovery time and process; it all comes down to how your body heals and the extent of the damage caused to your lung and body by the PE. In most cases the full recovery time is between one and two years. I remember it taking just over a year before I felt anywhere near as well as I had been before my PE.

This set me unknowingly off on what was to be my 'foodie entrepreneurial' journey. There are certain foods you have to avoid whilst you are taking blood thinners, as they can interfere with how the thinners work with your blood. This is mainly those which contain Vitamin K: green leafy vegetables, such as kale, spinach, broccoli, cauliflower, cabbage, green leaf lettuce, and cranberry, grapefruit, avocado, and soya. You get the picture: all the healthy delicious food and vegetables which I actually love and used to include in my diet.

So, I researched these foods and others, and gradually increased these back into my diet. By doing this, I was able to reduce the amount of medication I was taking, and over several months became medication free, which I still am to this day. Some people have to remain

Claire's Diamond

Once you have a deeper knowledge you can't go back – you can't unlearn what you've learnt – and this can be a blessing and a curse. It can lose you friends, it can make you restless, it can put you in scary places, totally out of your comfort zone... but listen to what you know in your gut. It's there for a reason, for you to figure out and follow.

on medication for life following a PE, and I was determined to do all I could not to be one of them.

What went through my mind was this: WHY DID I SURVIVE – WHAT IS MY PURPOSE?

I was faced with a challenge of trying to understand why I'd survived a life-threatening condition. It felt like I'd had an 'awakening' but what was I to do with it?

To this day I know my PE has changed me. I have ZERO tolerance to:

- Bullshit (I didn't have that much in the first instance, but now have none!)
- Time wasters
- Procrastination (although I am human, and have to kick my own arse from time to time)
- Merely existing
- Fake, meaningless people or conversations
- Living in comfort zones
- Settling for less than I KNOW I am capable of
- Not shouting up, and keeping my mouth shut when I know I should speak out
- Not living to the full
- Giving a fuck about unimportant stuff
- In summary, to not being in life 100%

Armed with this 'new me' (which by the way I am grateful for the experience of now, but at the time I was like 'why me', this is shit, life was good, stressful, but good, then the rug was well and truly pulled, what the actual fuck?!) I set out to think, what did I want to do? I had been a lucky one to be plucked from the hamster wheel and live to tell the tale, but not that lucky

Claire's Diamond

I believe you should adopt
these zero tolerances too to get
where you know you belong
and have the ability to get to
– you need to take that leap.

Claire's Diamond

Are you going to pluck yourself from your hamster wheel, or leave it to chance that you may not get lucky like I did (that's how I chose to see it anyway)? Life is very much about making the best of what you've got, no excuses, grasp that nettle with both hands and get on with it, whatever your 'it' may be, or take.

because to stay alive financially, as we (stupidly) knew no other way (ah yes, we are all only too aware how marvellous hindsight is), we survived on credit cards, and racked up thousands of £s' worth of debt whilst neither of us could work.

By this time it was 2007. I was fully recovered, although we hadn't managed to claw our way out of the debt we'd accrued. I had my health back and my newfound thirst for knowledge on all things health food and nutrition related, but I was confused about what I wanted to do.

I hadn't had a eureka moment through my illness, just a knowledge and gradual awakening that I wanted to change, but was unsure on how to go about it, and what that looked like. At this point I should mention that the supermarket retail scene wasn't the place we now know it in many ways, certainly not in as far as healthy snacking is concerned.

There were no dedicated healthier snacking categories, and crisps/snacks certainly where kids were concerned were dominated by Wotsits, Monster Munch and Quavers, with Pom Bears masquerading as 'healthy', although they were the preferred/only gluten-free option for many. That's about all (in my opinion) that could be called out there. I should also say at this point I am not a nutritionist, nor do I have any qualifications in nutrition, just a 'hands-on' understanding gained through my personal and business journey.

John and I had decided that we wanted to get into the food industry. We wanted to launch our own food brand. Our kids by this time were three, seven and nine years old, and following my near-death experience, I

Claire's Diamond

Health really is your first wealth, so put this first at any and all costs. It's all too easy to put this last, especially as entrepreneurs; we are a fast paced, sometimes wired bunch, who at times think we are invincible, but you can't talk your way out of ill health. Trust me, no one is listening.

was keener than ever to provide them with the best food I could and started to look at what they were eating and what was available to parents with kids of this age. This is when I took a good look at snacks and realised the scarcity mentioned above.

So, I shared earlier that I wasn't from the food industry, but also having no connections or knowledge of this it was a tough place to start from, and I think more so with us not being from London. London has such a wealth of resources, networks and a general foodie vibe, and I remember when I was starting to research feeling somewhat of an outsider, *a northerner on a mission who didn't fit in*. Not the case now, though. I have since learnt that they are the friendliest bunch, and I have made some great friends and connections along the way which has given me now, I am very honoured to say, a very influential network of professionals.

Where could we possibly start, I thought? My first 'proper' job was as a double glazing sales rep in the early 90s. Although it was brutal at times, it taught me many things, I think most importantly about myself, how not to give in, the true value of persistence (I believe persistence wins the day every time over even talent or knowledge) and to keep slogging at it, how to get round perceived objections from customers (yes, I was that pushy double glazing rep who didn't leave the house without a cash deposit and signed order form in my hands!), how to negotiate, and to better understand my own psychology: what makes me tick.

The most important thing it taught me about people, and what most probably helped shape me into the people person I am today, is just that: they are just people. They could be dressed in a suit, stay-at-home

---

Claire's Diamond

Nothing worthwhile in this life comes to you without bloody hard work, steely determination, perseverance and persistence, but here's the secret: these are the sweet spots, and as hard as it is at times, enjoy these experiences because they mould you, what you learn and who you become.

---

mums, buyers (in the case of my Scrubbys journey), bank managers, solicitors, you name it, underneath we/they are all the same and I soon realised that.

So, with my people approach, and hitting the streets mentality, we decided to take a regular pitch on a local market armed with other brands' products. We had decided that would be the ideal place to do our research, not only from a customer viewpoint (what would sell, what would they be drawn to from a branding aspect, what were they willing to pay), but to also get to know the inner workings of buying from a wholesaler. This was kind of taking a reverse engineered approach with the thought process that although we were their customers now, they would become our customers, and we needed to understand margins, processes etc.

I decided to take myself off to London to research what was selling, what was new in the 'foodie mecca', with the understanding that whatever works in the capital eventually makes its way up north. I must confess that as I was trawling the food halls of Harrods, Partridges, Fortnum & Mason etc, I was internally dreaming of when I could supply them with my product and see my brand on their shelves.

I had certain criteria which our product needed to meet. It needed to be:

- Healthy/something healthier
- Something which kids would eat
- Something new or different

Claire's Diamond

I believe there is no better place to test a product than a market stall; you get immediate direct feedback from your customers, good and bad, and you can learn so much which you might not otherwise learn, all of which is so valuable when it comes to buyers, when you reach that stage.

Other than that, we were open to most things, and we narrowed it down to

1. Juices
2. Soups
3. A snack item
4. A porridge bar with flax and other milled seeds in it
5. Healthier biscuits

We started to think about what we might want our brand to be called. We had been thinking for weeks with nothing really grabbing us. I firmly believe that the name of your brand can be make or break and therefore it needs a lot of time and thought applied to choosing this, especially given you can win awards for your brand, as we went on to do. More on that later, but really do think long and hard on your brand name.

One Sunday afternoon we sat down to think, and name after name, after name, after name, after name and mind-numbing thinking, I took a break to go make a cup of tea, and there it came to me while making that cuppa: Muddy Boot Foods. It fitted perfectly with all the ethics we had decided we wanted our brand to stand for – honest, earthy and innovative.

It was catchy; it wasn't wedded to a certain food type, and it was fun sounding, since all the product types we were looking at derived from being in mud and wearing boots!, so we set about getting the trademarks in place and developing the logo. We traded on the market stalls with this brand name for a few years.

When you register a trademark (www.ipo.gov.uk), you can either do this yourself or via an IPO representative firm. We elected to use a firm, Murgitroyd & Company, and I am pleased we did because we soon received one of our first challenges in what was to be the rollercoaster ride of our lives in the shape of launching a food brand: another company attempting to use our mark.

One day we received through the post a notification from Murgitroyd that another company was attempting to file and trademark a name which was so similar to ours it was beyond unscrupulous to even try. Our marks (registered in 2007) were MUDDY BOOT and MUDDY BOOT FOODS, and the one attempting to register was MUDDY BOOTS, and to add insult they were trying to register in three of the same classes we had our trademarks registered in.

The notification wasn't too much of a shock to me as one Sunday evening we were watching a programme called *High Street Dreams*, a BBC television documentary series based around the development of products to sell in high street shops and supermarkets, hosted by Jo Malone the British perfumer and Nick Leslau, an English commercial property investor, and there on the TV was a company with OUR name. I remember standing in our lounge having watched the programme and feeling gutted. How could I stop this, I thought?

I took advice from Murgitroyd who advised us it would cost thousands of pounds and time, as it could be contra-fought by them with the fact that in the three years since we had registered our marks we hadn't brought a product to market (we had been trading on our market stall, but did not have our own product). We just didn't have that kind of money to enter into such a process, so I started thinking.

I was due to attend the opening of a local business park, the premises for E-Factor, a business support group based in Grimsby, North East Lincolnshire (which would go on to play a most significant role for our business in the coming years, more than I realised) and Tim Campbell MBE, first winner of *The Apprentice*, was the keynote speaker. I went along and at the end of his talk he opened the floor to questions, and I was thinking about if/how we could fight the trademarking issue, so I confidently raised my hand and asked a question along the lines of, 'Do you know if in the IP world there is such a service as no win no fee, like you get no win no fee accident lawyers, do you know of anyone who could help me with an IP issue I have please?' I think he liked the fact that I had the balls to ask a question as the room was packed, and quite silent, so he invited me to talk to him more once he had wrapped up.

I spent a good half an hour talking with Tim, and he was so kind. He gave me the contact details of the lawyers he used in London, to contact and ask all I wanted, totally free of charge, and they would help me all they could. I was gobsmacked: here was a guy who

Claire's Diamond

There are no stupid questions, as we all know, only the ones you don't ask. Always have the courage to ask, and speak your truth. In my experience this has only led to positive outcomes.

had won *The Apprentice*, working with Sir Alan Sugar, and he was willing to help me out, nothing in it for him. I was so grateful and really taken aback that someone could help me so much.

The advice we received was much the same as Murgitroyd gave, although they did suggest that we could simply call the applicants directly, and try and negotiate with them.

John called them, and after a few phone calls and some back-and-forth, they agreed to withdraw their mark. Success... or so we thought. Then not too long later they re-filed with a slight adjustment to the mark, by adding their names underneath. Yes technically it was different, however in truth, they would still be recognised as Muddy Boots.

What to do now? My mind went back to something that Tim Campbell had said in his talk, something along the lines of 'When you're that fly hitting the window time after time, after time, there is a point where you have to stop flying at the window'. This felt like we were the fly, but I was unsure of what to do: keep our name, or move on? This would take time to think on, so we parked this and carried on with what we were doing.

One Saturday on the market stall a regional rep from a crisp company stopped by to speak to us on our stall. I need you to imagine here for a moment, if you will, the most amazing market stall you have ever seen: brightly coloured, fully branded, us dressed in tops with logos on them, hessian on the wooden stall surface. I. am. telling. you. our market stalls were ahead of their time: posters advertising the health benefits of certain products, vinyl banner at the front of the stall, fully branded; we looked the business!

Clearly the way we had presented the stall caught her attention. The conversation went along the lines of, 'Hi, I am from Burts Crisps, we're looking for stockists of our crisps, which includes our new mixed root vegetable crisps'. We were faced with a bit of a dilemma; crisps weren't exactly healthy, but we were still trying to clear our debts, three kids etc, so if we could stock a product on our stall which would sell well it couldn't be sniffed at.

Yes, you guessed what happened next; we started selling Burts. We also were selling exceptionally well (as the lady in the order centre told us each week when we rang in to place our order) on James White beetroot juice, so I made a duo buy for customers advertised with one of my blinding, glossy posters on the stand shouting out the health benefits of beetroot.

The juice and crisp combo was selling like hot cakes, however although my fancy poster shouted out how good beetroot was for lowering cholesterol, blood sugar, blood pressure, it very cleverly neglected to tell you that the crisps had circa 36g of fat per 100g, and I felt terrible. I had my loyal customers coming up to me telling me that they loved the vegetable crisps, and that the beetroot in particular (I was convinced it was my clever marketing skills that had something to do with it) was delicious.

So... it was there on that market stall in Beverley, East Yorkshire that the eureka moment arrived when I said to John, 'Do you think we can make these crisps healthier, and if so shall we launch our own crisp brand?'

Claire's Diamond

It's great to have principles, but they don't pay the bills. We all have ideals, but best to grow into those rather than burn what could be a great idea from the off for the sake of your principles.

Claire's Diamond

Trust your gut, no matter what;
that initial second in your gut
should not be ignored at any cost.

We are now in 2011, and we have been trading and selling our foodie wares on our Muddy Boot Foods market stall every Saturday and attending a few food fairs at weekends for around three years, learning so much about products, brands, wholesalers, customers, margins etc. We had settled on what we wanted our food brand and business to be, so now it was time to set wheels in motion.

I am very much the kind of person that, once I get an idea or decide on something in my head, I make it happen, no matter what. In this instance it was to meet Peter Jones at the MADE Festival in Sheffield. I had watched (as most of us, I am sure, have) *Dragons' Den*, and thought he would be great to get in front of if I could, and run my idea past him (on one hand I was crazy in a daft way: was this even possible? and on the other hand crazy in a good way; I believe as an entrepreneur you need a healthy dose of crazy). What was it Steve Jobs so rightly said?

"THOSE WHO ARE CRAZY ENOUGH TO THINK THEY CAN CHANGE THE WORLD USUALLY DO."

In my case my crazy idea was to make snacking healthy and I was to do this in the first instance through vegetable crisps, by launching a brand with a product range of healthy vegetable crisps.

Since our brand was called Muddy Boot Foods, we settled on calling our vegetable crisps Muddy Boot Roots, all felt good, and we were very excited with how things were heading.

At the time I researched every single business resource I could including shows and exhibitions to go to, and that is where I came across the MADE Festival in Sheffield and the knowledge that Peter Jones was one of the keynote speakers. Having decided I was going to meet him, now I had to figure out how exactly at a festival where thousands of people would be, and if/when I did, what exactly would my 'elevator pitch' be.

I needed a 'quirky' idea to present Muddy Boot Roots to Peter Jones with, so after much thinking I came up with making a gift bag, only a small clear cellophane wrapper one, which would contain:

- A posh individually wrapped biscuit
- A posh individually wrapped tea bag
- A business card I had made online via Vistaprint
- A printed leaflet on quality paper succinctly explaining my healthier snacking idea
- A handwritten note which read along the lines of: *'Hi Peter, really great to meet you today, thank you so much for your time. As a thank you, please enjoy a cuppa and a biscuit, and if you have a spare minute, it's be amazing if you could read the enclosed leaflet. Yours sincerely, Claire.'*

So, I had what I was to present to him all sorted... I just needed to figure how I was going to meet him. I was in a large function room at the festival listening to him on stage being interviewed. I was at the very back of the room, and there must have been at least 200 people in front of me. I was beginning to think I wasn't going to be able to complete my mission of meeting him, and I was wracking my brains as to how I could get to him.

I had seen the door at the far end of the room where he had entered the stage, so logic said he would exit by that door too, and using my hospitality knowledge of understanding the 'back of house' layout of function rooms, staircases, corridors etc, I took a rough guess as to where the door would come out. I found myself heading along a bedroom corridor. I had managed to get past a series of doors which were being guarded by hotel staff by literally blagging, trying to look 'important' and pretending to be on my phone – it worked!

So, I'm walking along the corridor, on my 'must meet Peter Jones mission', when a gentleman approached me, asked me who I was and what I was doing here. He was really nice, professional and friendly with a calm and 'knowing' air about him. I explained my healthy snacking idea, and that I was trying to meet Peter Jones. He confirmed I was on the right corridor, and that Peter would be around soon; he knew this as he was a keynote speaker too. Turned out this man was Wilfred Emmanuel-Jones, founder of The Black Farmer brand, and I had no idea!

Now before I knew who this very kind gentleman was, whilst I was explaining what I wanted to achieve with my brand and products, he gave me this gold nugget piece of advice: he told me to succeed with my brand I should **'be a disruptive influence'**, and this turned out to be one of the most important pieces of advice I received, and I will share throughout this book just how I used it, and what results I got from it.

I caught sight of Peter Jones out of the corner of my eye, gave my swift apologies to Wilfred Emmanuel-Jones that I had to leave, and cut our conversation off mid-flow to get in front of Peter. I caught him on the stairs as he was just about to leave one of the bedrooms where he was giving a press interview. I kind of 'pushed' past one of his 'people' and handed him my perfectly presented cellophane package containing all my hopes and dreams.

I never did get a conversation (or at least not then), or any interaction at all really; he just accepted the package and said thank you, and the next second, he was gone. I knew in my heart I wouldn't hear anything from him, and I think right there on the staircase I got a massive realisation that this journey wasn't going to be as plain sailing as I had naively told myself.

The Practical Stuff

So, you've heard what I did, how I got my idea, what ignited my entrepreneurial spark. Knowing what I do now, not only through my own personal experience, but also the many clients I have worked with launching their businesses, here is the process I recommend you follow when launching a (food) business. Let's get stuck into step 1 here.

STEP 1:
First Steps When You Have a Food Product Idea

Do you have an idea on the product you would like to launch?

The very first step is to embark on grass roots research. Not all ideas will turn out to be viable product options and there are various reasons for this. It could be around the production method, it could be around your proposed ingredients, it could be that you are unable to make, deliver and sell the product profitably, and it could also actually be about you.

Some clients I meet have hobbies which they 'think' they would like to turn into a business, but when all the finer points are drilled down, they actually realise that perhaps they'll leave the brownies to treating family and friends with rather than trying to accomplish world domination brownie style.

This is as important as anything; all things including you and your goals and wishes need to be thrashed out from the off. Rather know now than after you've invested your life savings or re-mortgaged your house.

What you need to establish is:

Is there a gap in market for it?

How did you get your idea? This may help you in your research. Did you think of your product when you tried something like what you are thinking of, and thought 'I could do this better'? Do you have or know someone with a food allergy/intolerance, and you want to solve a problem? Do you think a 'trend' is coming, and you can see a niche? There can be many reasons why you want to launch your food product. I recommend putting all of these down on a sheet of paper, or use the worksheet to follow at the end of this chapter. It will help you gain clarity.

What is the USP (unique selling point) of your product?

You need to differentiate what is unique about your product. Very few products/brands, if any, survive if they are simply a 'me too' product. New product development and innovation are the lifeblood to keeping ahead in the fast-moving industry of food. Behaviours, tastes, trends and demands change constantly so it's essential, in my opinion, to spend time on this aspect.

I would also recommend carrying out relevant research to find out if the product sector you are looking at is in growth or decline. What eating occasions will your product have? The more eating occasions you have attached to your product the more chance you will have of higher sales. For instance, Scrubbys could be eaten as a snack, with a dip, as canapes, as a side garnish to a sandwich, and even cooked in recipes such as nachos. How can you demonstrate the use/eating occasion outside of just the most obvious one which your product is?

If you copy a product, you may not have much longevity, as it may have launched when the category was growing and now be in decline. Your product should have something different/unique about it. If your initial idea doesn't have a point of difference, have a think about how you could make it different, i.e. cooking method, ingredient variation, health credentials etc.

Who will you target your product to?

Have a clear idea from the beginning who your target market is. This will be needed throughout the process of product creation, but also in your brand identity, sales and marketing of your product. There are some great resources now where you can test concepts and gain insights to back up who your target market might be, and test if they will buy your product. www.vypr.com is great for this.

Where will you sell your products?

Which route to market have you got in mind? This will vary depending on your product and target market. There are various routes which can be taken, not all of which rely on the big retailers (Tesco, Sainsbury's, Morrisons, Asda etc). These could include, but are not limited to:

- Farm shops nationwide: you can supply these direct or through distributors
- Delis and food halls: these are increasing in number, and as above you can supply direct or via a distributor
- Distributors: The Cress Co, Cotswold Fayre, Suma, Diverse Fine Foods, Marigold Health Foods etc.
- Foodservice: Brakes, 3663, Bidfood, Town & Country
- Fashion Retailers: Primark, New Look, River Island, Topshop
- Sports Retailers: Go Outdoors, independent sports shops, MuscleFood
- Discounters: Poundland, B&M, Home Bargains
- Online: Amazon, NOTHS (Not On The High Street), etc.
- Health Retailers: Holland & Barrett, Superdrug, Boots, and other pharmacies

As you move onto the next steps, production, ingredients and price of your product, the route by which you intend to sell your products will be hugely relevant so it's worth thinking through all the routes at this stage. It's a common misconception that the big retailers are the only, or most desirable, route to take.

Who are your competitors?

Carry out a competitor benchmarking exercise. You need to know who your product will be competing with. Whichever route to market, and these will most probably be multiple, the bottom line is you will be pitching to a buyer, trying to convince them to choose your product over another. Having all the information on your competitor and their products, as well as the category as a whole, will help you:

A – Make sure you're bringing something new/different to market.

B – Know where your competitors are retailing.

C – Demonstrate to the buyers that you are a serious player, and you know your category.

A benchmarking exercise is where you look at all the competitors in the category your product will enter.

Make a list of the sales targets you have; one could be Waitrose, for example. Find your competitors and make a spreadsheet like the one overleaf. Fill it in weekly and watch the activity in the category. This in time will tell you a number of things:

- You may get insights into when the category reviews are through seeing changes in what is listed.
- You will have an understanding of what promotions they run.
- You will see if the packaging size/ingredients change for any reason.

Example: the crisps aisle in Waitrose

Date & store	Brand & flavour	Bag size in grams	Price per bag	Price per gram	Promo yes/ no	What promo is
1st Jan	Scrubbys 4 Veg Mix	100g	£2.49	0.0249	No	N/A
8th Jan	Scrubbys 4 Veg Mix	100g	£1.99	0.0199	Yes	50p off

Are you passionate about your product?

One of the key things here is that YOU MUST BE PASSIONATE about your product. This passion and enthusiasm will be the fuel in your tank when things aren't going your way. If you are passionate about what you are doing, this will naturally translate through your business, brand and all your interactions, be they face to face if you are on a market stall or at a festival, but also when you are pitching to buyers. If you are not GENUINELY passionate you can't fool anyone, least of all yourself, and you will need your passion in bucketloads throughout your journey.

Real Account

HOW I'VE HELPED AND WORKED WITH A FOOD BUSINESS

A good gut feeling! (Geddit? Gut feeling? Probiotic yogurt?)

I had an idea... but with no knowledge of creating, making or launching a food product, all I had was a gut feeling that I might be onto something.

I needed 'someone on the inside' to confirm that not only was it a reasonable idea but that it was entirely possible to achieve.

A recommendation from a friend led to an initial chat with Claire and there was that gut feeling again, telling me that here was someone to show me the way. She clearly knew her stuff and her enthusiasm for the idea was infectious and inspiring. Claire and I worked our way through the project step by step:

- Research and product testing
- Proving the concept and finding a manufacturer
- Raising finance to launch
- Creating the brand
- Marketing plans
- Targeting, approaching and pitching to buyers

Without a mentor, the project would have been extremely daunting and I'm sure I would have taken many, many wrong turns but, because Claire had been along this path before, wrong turns and dead ends were avoided. She was able to clearly explain the preparation and execution of each step and how to overcome the inevitable obstacles. I've been known to call her a genius before and, although I don't want to be too dramatic, sometimes just by instinct she's able to come up with the most brilliant ideas and solutions.

On an emotional level, creating a brand is tough and it can seem a very lonely place. I've found that a mentor like Claire legitimises these emotions. Claire knows it's tough – she's been there, and she knows what to do to get through and get the job done.

A year or so on and The Veggie Plot is well on its exciting adventure, listed in Ocado and several independent retailers and wholesale distributors, and I still contact Claire for advice and support when I need it.

A mentor is not just for Christmas!

Anna Spencer | The Veggie Plot – Savoury Yogurts
www.theveggieplot.co.uk

What Would Claire Do Now?

Using the gift of experience I now have, what would I do differently in those early stages?

I would reach out and have a mentor from the off. This can be perceived as difficult due to cashflow restrictions, especially if you are starting from a minus financially as we were, but if there is any way at all you can do this I strongly advise it. The money you invest in a mentor/coach etc. can save you time and money.

You can also of course find a mentor who doesn't cost. For instance, I am a Virgin StartUp Mentor. If you choose to take out a start-up loan from Virgin, you are also provided with a mentor. This is on a pro bono basis. All mentors at Virgin provide their services on this basis.

To have someone external looking in to your business will not only help the business in terms of increased chances of success due to bringing in expert knowledge, advice and experience, but also depending on how your start-up is structured – sole, partnership etc. – it can provide that all-important person to bring perspective.

If you are on your own that's very daunting. If you are in a partnership, and that person is also your spouse or relative, it can put immense pressure on your relationship. I know and am willing to share, for the sake of others living through the same negative feelings and emotions that we at times did too, that working together and running a business together has the potential to finish your marriage or relationship.

We have been through hell and back. This not only affected us but our kids also.

I think that had we been able to 'offload' and share with someone external that would have helped tremendously. The pressure you face when you are starting a business, and in our case raising three kids too, is intense and all consuming.

With the best will in the world, whether you think you will or not, you will take those pressures and strains out on each other.

And though in this case I practised what I preach, I would also advise that whatever you embark on do it 100%. If you do something half-hearted that is exactly just what you will get back. What's the point in that? Do something you are interested in and passionate about. This way you will be more fulfilled and get the results.

Exercise:

What YOU should do now

What's my big idea?

Have I identified a gap in the market for it?

What is the USP to my product?

Who is my customer?

Where will I sell my products?

Who are my competitors?

CHAPTER 2

Birthing the Brand

Time was pushing on and we needed to knuckle down and write a business plan. Up until now we'd been researching, meeting our customers, examining competitors and gaining an understanding of the food industry.

All of this is equally as important; however, all we'd learnt needed to be put down in one document, to map out how exactly we were going to bring our product and brand to life.

Not having any idea on where to start with this, I used templates I'd found online. There's plenty out there; I've included some at the end of the book.

I know some people don't write a business plan, and we've all most probably heard stories of how the world's greatest entrepreneurs, Steve Jobs and Bill Gates, didn't have a business plan, and I'm not suggesting that you're not going to be the next Bill Gates, I hope you are, however they are exceptions, not the typical entrepreneur. I also think that having your business plan laid out as a 'blueprint' from the off helps in a number of ways:

- Essentially, you're making forward planning decisions: what you are hoping to achieve, how you are going to achieve your plans. It's your road map.
- You can see at a glance once everything is down if there are any glaring flaws in your plan.
- When any opportunities/distractions arise as your business develops, you can refer back and will have a better understanding of whether these are a good thing to pursue or not; you have already made the decision.
- If you choose to take a turn which wasn't in your original plan (which will most probably happen), you can project through further into your plan to see how it could potentially pan out.
- If you're looking for investment you will not get anywhere without one – FACT.
- Equally you may think you need investment (depending on your business), and perhaps discover you may not once you lay it all out, or you need more/less than you thought.
- It's a handy guide to keep you in check on where you are in line with your projections.

Part of our research was how we were going to produce our crisps. This led us to three production options: baking, dehydrating or vacuum frying.

This was by far one of the biggest challenges, as it is for all businesses which have a product. Our first decision was, do we manufacture ourselves, or do we outsource? This is THE question all foodie start-ups are faced with.

Claire's Diamond

Any road will do if you don't know where you're going, but you may well end up in the wrong place with the wrong business on your hands.

There are pros and cons to each route, and here are just some:

Own Manufacture

Pros

- Full control of supply chain
- You can scale up production as you grow
- If you are more passionate about manufacturing as opposed to innovating, you'll have more work satisfaction
- You can hold on to any recipe USP; less fear of your ingredients/recipe being copied
- You could white label to keep capacity on machinery sufficient (although you would have to ensure this didn't dilute sales from your brand)
- Tweak recipes/ingredient ratios faster and easier

Cons

- Costly set-up
- Higher probability of hiring staff from the off
- SALSA/BRC accreditations etc.
- Keeping up with regulations as and when they are introduced
- Less flexibility with location of your business
- Can be tied in for a long time to premises and lease agreements etc.
- If you don't have enough volume to push through, for financial demands you may need to white label for other brands, which can be a negative for your brand depending on how you did this.

Outsourced Manufacture

Pros

- More physical working time to sell and market your product
- All manufacturing legislation and regulations taken care of by the manufacturer
- Can assure retailers that high volumes from the off are no problem
- Less costly to start up
- You can trial your idea before jumping into premises costs

Cons

- Finding the facility in the first place
- You could be faced with high minimum order volumes
- The facility may close or stop wanting to supply you, leaving you with no manufacturer
- It can be costly to innovate new lines
- Your recipe/formulas aren't 'secret'
- You don't have as much flexibility and control

Some foodie entrepreneurs (most) start out in their kitchen, and that's certainly what we did. It's a low-cost way to prove concept, get some volume started, and refine your recipes/flavours.

You need to have your premises registered with your local council; here is where you start. It's a great resource for most information you will need: www.food.gov.uk.

There are industrial kitchens you can hire such as www.foodstarsuk.com; these may or may not be suitable depending on where you are based, and what equipment you need for whatever your product is. These weren't of use to us, as they didn't have the equipment we needed, plus we weren't London based, so we commenced research in other areas.

With knowledge of the three production method options, we drilled down into the full mechanics of each. We soon discounted baking once we'd run through the commercial aspect; the ratio of raw ingredients vs. finished product wasn't going to stack up financially.

Then we explored a dehydration method in more depth and discounted this too as we weren't happy with the taste profile from this method. We were able to achieve the health credentials we were aiming for: low fat, low calorie, however in our opinion they didn't taste great. **You can have the healthiest product in the world, but if they don't taste great no one will buy them.**

We were attempting to take the taste buds of the nation, whose only experience of vegetable crisps was circa 36g/fat per 100g and 500kCal+ per 100g, to a healthier destination, so trying to drag them too far the other way would, we imagined, be a stretch too far. We thought the best way was to take them on a healthier journey rather than cold turkey to out and out healthy which dehydrating would have given us.

This decision led us to explore the vacuum frying method more deeply. We came across vacuum frying after some intensive research which led us to connect with a gentleman we met over the internet, Akhilesh Pandey.

Akhilesh was completing a Master of Science degree in food production and had studied vacuum frying and written an entire 255-page thesis on it, so I knew we were in safe hands. He shared his thesis with us, which was amazing and gave us all we could have ever wanted to know on the subject. Vacuum frying ticked all the boxes of what we wanted:

- Cooks at a much lower temperature creating a product which has none of the burnt and oily overtones of vegetable crisps which were currently available.
- Creates a product which is much healthier, delivering lower calorific and significantly lower fat content: 35% less fat and 18% less calories.
- The frying process is carried out at circa 140 degrees as opposed to conventional frying at circa 180 degrees.
- The lower cooking temperatures result in significantly lower levels of acrylamide being produced in the product. Acrylamide is a chemical compound which forms naturally in certain food products when they are cooked at high temperatures. At high doses acrylamide has been known to cause cancer in laboratory animals. At the time of our research, the FSA, WHO and many other health regulatory bodies had not determined if the presence of acrylamides in food was a danger to humans and recommended that no change in diet was necessary, but studies are ongoing on the subject.

There has since been a fair amount of negative press about acrylamide in fried products, in particular crisps, which has called out the biggest players in the industry as having some of the highest acrylamide levels.

As I write this book there's new legislation coming into force later in 2018, whereby food businesses will be required to perform sampling and analysis to determine the level of acrylamide in foodstuffs and put in place steps to manage acrylamide within their food safety management systems. This will ensure that acrylamide levels are as low as reasonably achievable in their food.

Within Akhilesh's thesis were details about 'batch' vacuum fryers, smaller versions of the full-size vacuum fryers. The full-size fryers, continuous fryers, are approximately the size of an oil tanker, and the associated costs of setting up our own factory would have run to circa £2m.

Given we were just two people with historic debt still, a crazy dream, no knowledge of the food industry or food production, the full set-up wasn't an option. We concluded that we wanted to do the production ourselves with a batch fryer and would upscale as volumes increased by adding more batch fryers.

We bought the vegetables we'd decided to use: carrots, beetroot, parsnips and sweet potatoes, and a mandoline to thinly slice the vegetables, and baked the slices in the oven. This was a very much 'prove the concept' mission; there was nothing new and innovative about doing this, because there were recipes and instructions on the internet.

Baking vegetable crisps at home for home consumption is one thing; creating a healthier vegetable crisp for a retail market that didn't exist yet was quite another, but we needed a product to start 'pitching' our idea with.

We knew we'd need to seek investment to get our idea off the ground. We had no money and were still trying to claw back from a minus financially, and not succeeding at any speed.

Remember I told you about E-Factor? Well here is where they started coming into play. We'd met with them, pitched our idea with our baked prototypes to access help from one of their advisors, and were successful. We ended up with a team of support: Mark, Julie and Tim.

I started to research events/places to meet potential investors and came across a group called YABA (Yorkshire Association of Business Angels). There was an investment seminar being held in Sheffield by YABA, so I applied for us to pitch.

I went along to another seminar hosted by YABA a few weeks earlier in Birmingham as a spectator to get an idea on how pitching worked:

- What did entrepreneurs pitch for in terms of £?
- What equity did they offer?
- What exit plans did they have in mind?
- What exit did potential investors look for?

All of this was new to me; I was a fish out of water in the biggest sense of the expression. I wasn't nervous, though. I am a very confident person by nature. I knew my subject from every aspect: our customers, our route to market, the production method.

All of these are what you absolutely need to have 100% unfaltering knowledge of when you embark on launching your food product. What I wasn't adept at was the 'investor' aspect; I'd never pitched to investors before.

The agenda came through for the investment seminar at Sheffield, and we were third up. I was doing the pitching and felt confident. I knew my product idea inside out, had a solid business plan and all the facts and figures which would be needed. What I wasn't prepared for, though, was the (negative) reaction to our healthy snacking idea.

We'd carried out so much research into healthy snacking, including working with Hull University and the HONEI Project (Humber Obesity, Nutrition, Education and Innovation). This was with the intention of targeting the product in helping the fight against obesity/dietary problems/health issues brought on by high fat and salt content in this food sector (snacks).

We'd had numerous meetings (with all three kids in tow) with members of the HONEI team including a nutritionist and a food technologist. Whilst we still had a long way to go with product development the feedback from this suggested there was no reason why the products would not be viable to produce.

Dragging the kids along with us to most of the meetings was an added challenge, and at the time I felt guilty having to do this. Now, on the other side of it looking back, I can see many ways in which it's taught them skills they need in life: confidence, meeting people, the ability to hold conversations, manners... the list goes on.

When doing public speaking, I often get asked by working mums facing the same guilt trip, either putting their kids in childcare more than they'd like, or, like me, dragging them everywhere, how I dealt with feelings of guilt?

Well, firstly if it's all your kids have known then the bad feeling is yours alone, and they know no other, so don't beat yourself up. Secondly, it's fascinating what you teach your kids without even knowing you're doing it. What they learn through seeing you do things is something I had totally overlooked. Thirdly, they will be so proud of you, seeing you working and trying; they have a deeper understanding of life, and I don't think anyone could argue about that only being a good thing.

This was 2011, and healthy snacking wasn't a concept back then. I was utterly convinced it was the way forward, but not everyone held that opinion, or was open to the possibility that it was going to be as we know it today.

The YABA pitch went well. I was:

- Prepared
- Calm
- Full of conviction
- Passionate

There were no curve ball questions to throw me. The only comments and question I was unable to defend was the resounding opinion in the room that no one wanted healthy snacks.

The common thought amongst the gentlemen was that no one would buy our lower fat, lower salt, healthier snacks. A snack was supposed to be an indulgent treat, therefore salty and high fat. So, we were wished well, but no, no one wanted to invest.

Here's the summary of what it soon became clear were the obstacles/opinions we would face time after time after time:

- No one wants healthier snacking, therefore it will never work.
- You're not from the food industry.
- You have no experience of the food industry.

There will be more times than not on your entrepreneurial journey where you'll face obstacles and opposition. That's just how it is. At first, in the very early days, these would shake me and set me off on a downward spiral of an 'I'm shit at life' thought process. I would convince myself that I was alone in all these struggles, and everyone else had it plain sailing, and it was just me who wasn't getting it right somehow.

This is why I now wholeheartedly believe that **YOU CANNOT DO THIS JOURNEY ALONE**; you need a support system, a team around you if you are to realise your goals.

On the other hand, some days I would fight back harder, totally sold on the belief that

**'People who say it cannot be done
should not interrupt those who are
doing it.' – George Bernard Shaw**

At the bottom of our business plan I had this quote:

**'Let food be thy medicine and medicine
thy food.' – Hippocrates, 2500 years
ago, the father of medicine.**

And I still believe this to this day. After all, I had firsthand evidence of the power of nutrition and healthy eating. I am still passionate about functional food and believe this will always be the underpinning of food innovation.

And consumers are waking up to this more as time goes on. It would seem, though, as far as these investors were concerned we were just ahead of our time.

So back to the drawing board in terms of cash to launch with. I was growing very weary; we were trying so hard and simply not getting any nearer to making our dream happen. Throughout every entrepreneurial journey we're all faced with times like this, and sometimes daily.

Life will push you as far down as you are willing to be pushed. Only you know your limits, how far you're willing to go, how much you will take before you decide to fight back. It is unique to everyone, so you can never compare, but this is so easy to do and then you can find yourself falling into victim mentality.

You may have friends or family who think you're stupid for taking so much on, or on the flip side, you may know people who stand up and fight way sooner than you. There is no right or wrong; you must have faith and trust that all is happening for a reason. What you learn from even the darkest places (these dark places are often the ones which reward you the best) is all better equipping you for what you'll need on your journey.

It's really tough fighting back. It takes all the strength you have, and you have to dig deeper than you have ever gone before, but believe me, when you do stand up to life, have that courage, self-belief, determination and conviction to say no more, to say 'I am good enough' and 'I can do it', you will turn the corner.

There'll be multiple corners, but here's the thing, life is really clever at giving you what you need when you need it.

I know from personal deep dark moments that life can feel unfair and confusing in the moment when things are coming thick and fast, and you **seriously wonder what the fuck, what now, why?**

When you look back you see the why – and in most cases, can be grateful of it, as what we are taught through experience we never lose.

Our next port of call (the final one in my mind as we had exhausted all avenues) for funding was through an introduction brokered for us by E-Factor to a local chamber funding facility, the Acorn Fund. This fund provides financial support to business start-ups unable to find funding from traditional sources.

We qualified for this due to our bad debt status. I was losing heart; we'd been trying for what seemed like forever, and often it was feeling like our dream was over before it had even begun. I remember saying to John on New Year's Eve 2011 that if we didn't find the funding to launch by the end of January then we should call it a day... move on. Accept that we had done our best and it wasn't meant to be for us.

We'd been through so much since my PE in 2005: my recovery; the kids growing up (they were now 7, 11 and 13); working regular day jobs whilst trying to get Muddy Boot Foods off the ground with markets and festivals every weekend and fighting through debt.

Our debt situation had taken us to all-time lows of bailiffs at our door, having our personal items levied. I believe we'd been taken as low as you could go; at one point my aunty and sister had to food shop for us when we were at our very lowest.

To this day I've never failed to be surprised at the goodwill of people; what you give out you really do get back. Throughout this book you will read instances of this: magic in motion. When a bailiff was trying to take John's truck I attempted to take him on, and was swiftly wrestled to the ground. What upset me most was the kids saw it all. It was heartbreaking for them to see their mummy so helpless. My neighbour across the road saw too, and rang us, and my defensive first reaction was that they were being nosy.

Claire's Diamond

Stress does this to you: makes you read situations and people wrong. It's hard but try your hardest to not be this way. Don't let external stress and pressure turn you into a monster that you're not.

My neighbour offered to help, but I said he couldn't possibly. He told me that I was in deeper than I realised taking the bailiff on; he was a bare-knuckle fighter and my neighbour had seen him fight.

'Let me help you Claire,' he said. After I'd wrestled with my pride and put it aside, not really having an option in reality, my neighbour came and squared things with the bailiff. We were eventually able to pay them back and I am grateful to this day for their help.

Where does the will to carry on come from? Where does that extra ounce of self-belief, determination and fight come from? I think it's from having courage and really understanding and accepting that what else are you going to do, just give in? Lie down? Accept defeat?

In any situation like this I think to myself, if this is how it was going to end, it would be the end, but it's not the end, I'm still here, I'm still fighting, therefore, it's not the end... so it's time to try harder, never say never, knuckle down, keep believing, and dig deeper than you ever have.

All that you go through happens for a reason: to give you all you need for the journey ahead, to help others, and to shape you into a better person.

Having had no success raising investment so far, we drilled further down into our proposed business model. Could there be a way to get it off the ground for even less money? Could we find a third-party manufacturer rather than run to the expense of the batch vacuum fryer set-up?

Claire's Diamond

Who have you ever met that created anything worthwhile, that had it easy and hasn't failed at times? Not had shit thrown at them? No, didn't think so, you haven't, nor have I.

We revisited the thesis from Akhilesh and found details of the manufacturers of the continuous vacuum fryers. We contacted them to ask where the nearest factory to us with a vacuum fryer was; it was the Netherlands.

We contacted the factory and they told us (and much to our bad timing) they'd just signed up with a intermediary company in the UK, giving them the licence in the UK for vacuum fried vegetable crisps.

This news led us on what we felt could be a wild goose chase to Borehamwood to meet with the company. Absolutely nothing came to us without having to jump through hoops; the hoop in this instance was wondering how the hell we were going to get ourselves to a meeting which involved a 320-mile round trip, six hours away, in a clapped-out car with three kids in tow?

We were down to our last £10 and wondering if we had enough fuel to get there and back. I elected to put the kids in childcare, but that was £60 for the day. Luckily, we had an account with the nursery, so could figure out how to pay that in a week or two.

Off we went to Borehamwood. I'd researched the company, and it turned out they were a multi-million £ turnover business, so that felt quite daunting. We were armed with our research, not quite knowing what the meeting would bring, although essentially we wanted to understand if we could be supplied product from the factory in the Netherlands, and associated costs.

At this stage we still hadn't raised the start-up investment, so were in the truest sense of the saying 'faking it until you make it' in the meeting. We explained all our research, how we'd sell the crisps, what we'd do to raise awareness etc. Essentially selling ourselves as best we could to try to secure an agreement with them. It felt this was our only hope of bringing this to life now we had the realisation we wouldn't be able to batch fry ourselves through funding restrictions.

We'd shared our ideas with them to try and convince them to work with us, with no reassurance that they wouldn't just take these, leaving us high and dry.

The meeting went surprisingly well; I remember coming out frustrated as hell though. These people were sat there with an agreement, having just pipped us to the post in getting to the factory, and now we'd have to pay them an extra 5% for that privilege, IF they decided they'd supply us.

We were back and fro for a few weeks and eventually came to an agreement, which was amazing in the sense that we had a route to bring the dream to life now. The added challenge we had, along with the vulnerability of the Euro (we were to pay the factory in Euros) was having to pay an extra 5% to this company too, which we knew would leave us with very tight margins.

E-Factor had helped us secure the meeting with the Acorn Fund, and we'd arranged to meet at the Enterprise Village, the same place we met Tim Campbell (I took this as a good omen). We went along with crisps made in our kitchen stored in an old Walkers shortbread biscuit tin.

As I felt that this our last and only chance left to secure start-up investment I wanted everything to be perfect. We arrived early to set the room up, and re-created our market stall in the room. We had a fully comprehensive business plan complete with commercials and projections.

We weren't pitching for as much now we wouldn't be manufacturing ourselves, and we'd calculated that if we could raise a £50k loan we could launch, so that's what we were going to pitch for.

I was in the final throes of setting the room up perfectly when the man from the Acorn Fund walked in. He hadn't been seated at reception and shown upstairs as was the plan; he just arrived in the room abruptly.

He looked quite intimidating in a long black overcoat, with a stern expression on his face. I wasn't ready for him; we hadn't got everything just right. I was on the back foot and not comfortable with that. But we carried on; there was no other option, and I did what I felt was a good pitch.

We were told that he (Peter) would be in touch in the next few days with his decision. Those few days were extremely long. Remember I'd told myself and John that if we didn't get funding by the end of January then we should call it a day seeing that we were gaining pace into January already.

I got the decision call from E-Factor. I was told that Peter from the Acorn Fund had called to say our idea wasn't for him, and like so many we'd met along the way, he wished us well but that was that.

I was absolutely devastated. Why was this so hard? Why at every corner we turned did we hit a brick wall? What were we to do now? I couldn't accept the no... I wasn't going to accept the no. I called E-Factor back

Claire's Diamond

Sometimes you have to go completely against the grain. Fuck the status quo; if you want it, really want it, nothing or no one can stand in your way; turn your power up.

and begged them to get us another meeting with Peter. This was successful, and booked in for a few days' time.

Before we had the second meeting, I had by chance gone to a meeting at Hull's World Trade Centre, networking, still trying to give this business life. I love to network. You never know who you're going to bump into. Who knows who. Don't they say you are only ever six degrees of separation away from anyone you want to meet?

That's a crazy scary thought, but yes, it is true. If you think for a second about your network and who you'd like to meet, you will surprise yourself. Brokering the meeting might be tough, but at least you know the route. Knowing the route, the 'how to', is always half the battle in all you set out to achieve as an entrepreneur – but that's what we are good at: finding a way and making it happen.

After the meeting at Hull's World Trade Centre I decided to call in to the Costa nearby. I was stood in the queue, and standing next to me was Peter, someone who a few weeks earlier would have been a complete stranger. I couldn't believe my eyes. As things stood I had no idea what he'd been told by E-Factor. Yes, clearly, he knew I'd requested a second meeting, but what he was expecting I didn't know.

Peter asked if I wanted to sit with him. I felt a bit nervous, but he wouldn't have been aware of this. I felt nervous because I knew how many avenues we'd gone down trying to secure investment. How long we'd been trying, and in my mind, he was our last hope and I was desperate to make a good impression.

Our conversation didn't turn into the business model grilling I'd expected. Yes, we chatted about it a bit, but also just chatted about life in general. I concluded he was a nice guy and the impression I first had of him being stern with a daunting demeanour couldn't have been more wrong. This was an example of what I'd learnt from my double glazing sales rep days: don't judge a book by its cover.

The day to present to Peter again was here. Back once again to the Enterprise Village. This time the presentation went better; I think this was in part due to meeting Peter randomly in Costa that day. I felt more at ease, and that I was able to talk him more openly. Looking back, I think my passion came through more. I did the pitch of my life; I put my heart, soul, dreams and everything I could muster into it.

We'd once again gone armed with crisps baked in our kitchen, and just as happened last time, all the crisps were enthusiastically chomped through. We'd brought a separate batch for Peter to take away with him this time. Along with the additional biscuit tin full of our baked prototypes he asked for copies of our business plan and commercial projections, which we gladly gave him. This felt like a good sign; he hadn't requested as much the previous time. Peter thanked us for our time, and as before said he'd be in touch soon.

A long agonising wait ensued again. We were now days from the end of January, my self-imposed deadline. Peter contacted us himself to give us the news; I couldn't believe my ears when he said that his decision was to give us the £50k loan we'd applied for.

Claire's Diamond

There will be moments. Decisions.
Turning points. Conversations.
People. Situations. That
change the course of your life,
your business. This was a key
defining one for us. Always
remember them; they are a good
barometer to check yourself
against as life moves on.

I kept it together on the phone, just, but after the call I sat and cried, happy tears, tears of relief.

All those years of hard work, all those market stalls, all that dragging the kids here and there, all those freezing cold mornings and all those pitching sessions for funding to launch had yielded a return. This was massive, and as the journey reveals in the coming chapters, this was to be one of the momentous days in our warp speed journey of launching our food brand.

We were elated, over the moon, totally deliriously happy. We'd done it! We had the funds to bring our dream to reality and could put our full energies into getting this off the ground.

To date John and I had our respective day jobs and were working on this at weekends and evenings. The very thought of not having to do this anymore and give this the rocket fuel in the form of all our time and attention was the most amazing feeling.

One challenge we still hadn't addressed was our brand name issue. What to do about the imposter 'Muddy Boots'? They'd since got launched into Waitrose with burgers. Waitrose was clearly a target retailer of ours, and I felt that it would be an obstacle not only with the buyers, but consumers too. I didn't want any confusion on what Muddy Boot Foods stood for; we were healthier snacking, not burgers.

I spoke to John, and told him that I thought we should change the name of the brand.

Admittedly the timing wasn't brilliant; we had just secured the funding. However, on the other hand the

Claire's Diamond

No matter what the consequences are, or what you perceive them to be, you must remain true to yourself. If you don't you will be on the run forever.

timing WAS brilliant. Any changes needed to be made now before we set off on the path with the brand.

So, it was agreed, let's change the brand name. What followed was 48 hours of inventing a new name. We wrote down a list of words that could be associated with the product. These included the vegetables, the cooking process and aspirations for the brand.

We only had this time frame as we'd got a meeting booked with Peter to sign for the loan cheque, and I didn't, after all the hard work getting to this point, want any obstacles getting in the way.

How's the saying go? 'There's many a slip twixt the cup and the lip.' I wasn't about to give any reason for things to be delayed, so the pressure was well and truly on.

We called my mum for any words she could think of, and we sat down with the kids. After all they'd been involved so much to date, so it felt only right that they had input too. They got quite involved and were enthusiastic about helping.

After intense hours of us all throwing our two-penn'orth in, voila, Scrubbys was born. We created the brand name using 'scrub' as in the production process (the vegetables are 'scrubbed' rather than peeled), and decided to add the 'by' from our family surname 'Brumby'.

Our tag line we settled on was 'Vegetable Crisps with Character'. This had multiple layers of meaning to it:

- The lower fat credentials
- The lower calorie credentials
- The lower acrylamide statistics
- We also wanted to expand the range at some point to include a children's line in which the vegetables were to become 'characters'

We of course did our homework on the trademarking aspect. We checked to see if 'Scrubbys' was available in the classes we wanted to register in, and thoroughly checked the word out in general. The only food product was an Australian wine, so we felt confident that we'd be ok in terms of trademarking without any opposition.

We also contacted some designers we'd met along the way when we'd been seeking advice on packaging design ideas for Muddy Boot Roots. I wasn't expecting the barrage of negativity the name 'Scrubbys' would get from these designers. How they felt the negative connotations of 'scrub' would hold the brand back. Good job I refused to listen to them. We went on to be awarded 'CoolBrands' status not only once but twice: in 2013/14 AND 2016/17.

We met with Peter, explained to him that our brand was now called Scrubbys, and the rationale behind that. He understood, agreed completely and also commented that he liked Scrubbys better.

Claire's Diamond

It's really hard sometimes to listen to what you believe to be right especially when so-called experts are telling you something other. You need to develop the ability to drown out their opinion and noise and listen to yourself.

Sat at the board table we completed all the paperwork, once again back at the Enterprise Village. That felt strange; here we were in the same room where I had months earlier been asking Tim Campbell for advice, not having secured any start-up investment and under pressure from a trademarking viewpoint, and now here we were signing paperwork to receive our long-awaited loan.

We were handed the cheque: £50,000.

We were in shock. I recall John and I driving away from the meeting with Peter and pulling over onto the side of the road. We just looked at each other. We'd achieved our goal of raising the start-up funding just one day from my deadline. We took a picture of the cheque; this was it: all we had been toiling to achieve to get this business launched had happened... we were on our way.

I wonder what I would have thought back then if someone could have played me a video of what the coming years were to bring, good and challenging. Actually, scrap that thought... some of the scenes would have been too scary.

Now we had the cheque it was time to find a bank to open an account. Remember the terms of securing funding from the Acorn Fund were that you had to produce evidence from a high street bank that you couldn't get funding. This was no problem for us given our bad debt status; not only were we unable to get a loan, they wouldn't give us a bank account either. This was the case with every single high street bank.

Peter had recommended a bank called Handelsbanken, so we went along to meet with the local bank manager. That was another lengthy meeting, presenting our business plan and financial forecasts. Handelsbanken are different in that they are more 'old school', true local relationship managers offering a bespoke relationship management service. This was just what we needed because if we were to be judged on credit ratings alone we'd never have been able to open a bank account.

After running credit checks the decision was that they would give us an account, no facility, but an account. Thank you very much. That was all I needed: a place to bank the cheque and crack on with getting on with the business of launching this brand. At long last it seemed all was coming together.

Boom... we were in business, and officially the only independent vegetable crisp company in the UK (other companies were producing vegetable crisps, but they were secondary to potato crisps). More importantly, more than that, **we were the only lower fat healthier vegetable crisp company in the UK.**

Here's where the real hard work was going to start...

The Practical Stuff

So now you're ready to move on to step 2 in my 8-step process:

STEP 2:
Bringing the Idea to Life

Now you've done your research, you've decided what your product is going to be, you're all fired up with passion and that fire in your belly, now it's time to bring your idea to life.

Business plan

It's a must that you write your business plan, and it's required for numerous reasons:

- You get all your ideas, mission, business structure down.
- It's essentially the 'blueprint' for your business.
- It helps to keep you on track with your 'why'... why did you decide to launch your business?
- It's good to look back on throughout your journey to remind yourself of your intentions and goals.

There'll be times along your journey when external 'opportunities' or decisions are thrown at you; invariably the answer will already be in what you wrote in your plan from the off; it helps keep you in line with your business goals.

I have clients who come to me whilst they are at start-up stage and don't have a plan of any sort in place. All too often they are focusing on what I call the 'exciting bits' like how they will market their products and they get lost in their own 'hype' of what they are creating.

Now I'm not dampening any fires here; you know from what I've already shared that passion is super important, but it's all too easy to get distracted here and skip the steps which are required at the time they're required, so please don't be tempted to rush on and jump over essentials which you really must have in place.

Have you got the cash required to launch?

With your business plan written and within it the necessary commercials associated, you will know what capital you need to launch.

- Do you have this?
- Will you need to raise some investment?
- If so where?

Thorough thought also needs to be given to how you will live and pay your personal bills whilst your business is growing. Are you going to 'hold down a day job' too whilst you get your business started, or does your food business need to pay you from the off? If this is the case do you have the cashflow required, bearing in mind timescales involved in gaining sales?

All the above needs nailing before you launch your business.

Do you have all the skills needed?

You have the passion, you have the product idea, and you now need to look at yourself, and your skill set (be brutally honest) and evaluate what you need help with, and where you can find the help.

There are many skilled areas within running your food business (as with any other business) that you will need to call on professionals for. Here are some of the basics you will need.

Where will they come from?

- Finance and accounting
- Purchasing
- Sales
- Marketing
- Production
- Logistics

If you, like me, are starting out on your own (it was my husband and I, but that was all) you have no other choice, certainly in the very early days, other than to do everything yourself. This will have benefits and consequences.

Where can you reach out for skills?

There are lots of groups and places, both online and through networking, where you can reach out for help and resources once you have highlighted where you need assistance. You will find some helpful resources for this at the back of this book.

Do not try to do everything yourself; you'll end up doing a bit of everything, and all of nothing!

You and your business will suffer, so nail from the off what you need and what it will cost. A mentor is someone who can be invaluable to you and your business.

Time frame?

Do you have a launch date in mind? Depending on where you intend to retail your product you can research an optimum time to launch, e.g. around reputable industry trade shows, or within a 'season' depending on your product's ingredients, or time of year.

It's always handy to have a launch date in mind, and work back from this, as it keeps you running to a deadline, and helps coordinate and focus you. Plans without action are futile. Remember my funding deadline!

When I work with my clients who are at start-up stage, I often use a trade show as a deadline, often via www.specialityandfinefoodfairs.co.uk as they have a section dedicated to new producers, The Discovery Zone. This is where I first exhibited with one of my clients, The Veggie Plot. They struck gold at this show with the Ocado buyer.

If your route to market is farm shops, delis, distributors or the multiple retailers, most of, if not all the buyers you'll want to get in front of will be at this show so it's a good one to attend. It has been running for 18 years or so now, so it has a good pull in terms of buyers. This was one of the very first shows I exhibited at with Scrubbys and I had the good fortune of catching a Waitrose buyer's eye.

Don't be too heavy on yourself though. The timeline is there to bring you focus; remember only you know the deadline you are imposing on yourself. If you need to flex on it slightly that's fine. Remember you only get one shot at making the first impression, so get it right!

Real Account

HOW I'VE HELPED AND WORKED WITH A FOOD BUSINESS

One of Junius's founding partners had the pleasure of seeing Claire present at a food entrepreneurs event in 2017. Claire was by far the standout guest speaker.

Claire's refreshing honesty regarding her own foray into bringing a brand to market was inspiring, and most welcome to a fledgling business such as ours. It was obvious that we had to meet with Claire one-on-one to tap into her invaluable insights. Our first meeting marked a defining moment in shaping our business strategy and taking our brand to the next level.

After presenting our concept to Claire, we were thrilled at how genuinely excited she was about where our brand could go. This was tempered with a compassionate slice of reality, of where and how things can and do go wrong, an ever-present concern for any business.

We have engaged with Claire since early 2017 and view her as a mentor and friend. We have been so grateful for the 'can we touch base today?' Skype calls and face-to-face brainstorming sessions. We always feel assured and more fired up after our meetings.

Having set up a great deal of focus groups, at Junius we had affirmation that there was a hole in the market for the time-poor health-conscious worker to choose health on the go. Above all, our food was nutritious and delicious but at Junius we wanted to simplify lunch logistics and work towards building a healthier workplace.

Two of the founding members both have master's in nutrition, and had clear insights into the daily health challenges that face the average corporate worker.

At Junius our business is the intersect between food, science and education but how did we get it out there and in an understandable way? Health focus groups shone a light on the delivery of delicious pre-packaged food and drinks, empowering employees to make health-motivated food choices whilst on the go.

The real challenge in our business was to bridge the gap in our knowledge between what we knew was needed and how to deliver it effectively with minimal cash burn. The hurdles were immense and numerous. Trying to break down costs, clearly pinpoint points of leverage and importantly get to grips with hospitality and retail terms became the hurdle at the outset.

Some of the challenges included:

- Hospitality and retail terminology
- Costings in general
- Logistics
- Brand alignment
- Manufacturing

These are singular terms but what Claire brought to us was a depth of knowledge, padding out each of these terms, which brought a three-dimensional understanding to our business. She brought life to the numbers but more than this, her intuitive brilliance, advice and guidance has been pivotal to getting us where we are today.

Funnily enough, we have come across many hurdles and it is that moment when the founders (we are a small family business) look at each other and say, 'Shall we ring a friend?' and Claire is the go-to person.

Working with Claire has been a sheer delight.

Her honesty, integrity and pure grit shines. What strikes us more about Claire, is her incredible intuitive nature... she is known to close her eyes in a mindful way and come back in a corporate way with a visceral reply, which never fails to be the correct advice.

Claire is a true and real sounding board and will, we hope, be part of the Junius journey in the future.

Junius | The Science of Food
www.wearejunius.com

What Would Claire Do Now?

Using market research as part of your business plan will help you determine how viable your business idea is, as well as helping convince potential investors further down the line, should you go down that route – this is something I got 100% right.

Market research shouldn't just be used when you are planning your business. You should do this on a regular basis to gain a deeper understanding of how your consumers and market are changing. This is something I did very well also. The markets, festivals and food fairs were where we conducted consumer research, but I also carried out a lot of retailer research as I shared with you in Chapter 1.

Using the gift of experience, what would I do differently in these early stages?

Don't launch underfunded.

Essentially, we'd cut the loan amount down so low to convince potential funders to invest the start-up capital we needed. This was a huge mistake, as we were cash-strapped from the off.

The truth is that it will take you three times longer than you think to get a volume of sales coming through and cost you three times as much in terms of cashflow – THE LIFE BLOOD OF YOUR BUSINESS.

You must have patience – there is an art, which if you develop will save your sanity a lot on this journey. Know when to dial up or down your patience levels. You need to know yourself pretty well to do this.

Ask yourself the question, does this situation require me to kick ass and get my impatience on – or do I need to chill out, and let the stress monster have a nap? Both are required in equal measures, and you will learn which situations need which approach.

Our sales projections were completely hockey stick. You must be realistic with these; you are only causing pain for yourself by over-egging them. Ours had unrealistic projections like the diagram on the left. Make sure yours are more aligned to the right diagram.

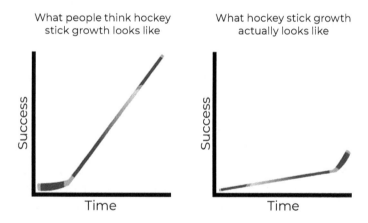

I would also ask yourself where your passion is: are you happy with the roles which are playing out for yourself in the business? If you are not happy then you and your business will suffer, and after a time you will come to resent the work you are doing.

Claire's Diamond

You must be honest with yourself at every stage of your journey. If you compromise and compromise, before you know it you are a mile off where you started, and that can be hard/ impossible to pull back from.

Exercise:

What YOU should do now

Business plan – Find a template you like and write your business plan. Jot down here any resources you've found.
Cash to launch – Do you need investment or a loan? If so write here where you may explore.
Skills – What skills are required in my business? Who will do what? What do I need to bring in?
Time frame – Write below the time frame you'd like to achieve and desired deadlines.

CHAPTER 3

Getting off the Starting Blocks

*N*ow we'd got the loan funding, our product and manufacturer secured, we needed to start working on brand design, packaging and a website.

I knew the brand design was going to be one of THE most important aspects. I knew this through all the research I'd carried out around other brands, but also with my face-to-face experience at the market stall. I set about contacting designers, and knew what I wanted, but my idea and what some designers were capable of producing were a world apart.

Hand on heart, we must have met and rejected around 10 designers; some of them didn't come up with anything better than my kids could have produced and quoted in excess of £1000 for the pleasure of producing a (rubbish) bag design.

Still trying to find a good designer, I was trawling through Google and came across a design agency in Lincoln; their website caught my eye. The animated cartoon character on the screen that was whistling

---

Claire's Diamond

The devil is in the detail; you must drill down to the last detail in all you undertake, and not cut any corners. If you do it's kind of like Monopoly: you will not pass go, you will not collect your £200 for passing go, you will get nowhere.

---

away had real life to it. It was different to all I had previously seen, and I had a good feeling about them.

We met with the design agency in Lincoln. Vicki understood what I wanted straight away. In fact, during the meeting as we were talking she started drawing what was to be our finished bag design.

We left the meeting and I felt so sure that they (Vicki) would come up with a winner. I remember driving home down the A15, and the Red Arrows who flight train there sometimes did a fly-by, and today was one of those occasions; it felt like this was just for me, like they were in approval of my good feeling about Vicki.

A few days later the email came through with her initial thoughts, and I was blown away. It was that good that I remember thinking it already looked like an established brand, like it already existed. I couldn't believe it was mine. My brand.

We elected to choose purple for the logo as this was in line with the brand personality we'd decided we wanted. There are 'regal' connotations to the colour purple, and we knew our crisps/brand were to be premium, so the purple made perfect sense. The icon for the Scrubbys logo was chosen because it is indicative of root vegetables growing and thriving out of the ground.

The icon grows from the title 'Scrubbys' which had a quirky but 'established' typeface to give a strong foundation for the elaborately decorative icon above it.

I loved the grounded, vintage, yet almost ethereal look it had. Whether standing alone as an icon or incorporated

Claire's Diamond

Clearly visible and unashamedly bold – that is how we all need to be when launching a product/ brand. Especially in the food world, there is no place for shrinking violets. If you are not seen you are not bought.

into our literature, the Scrubbys visual identity would be clearly visible and unashamedly bold.

All our research led us to decide on launching with two bag sizes, 40g and 100g. The packaging needed to be designed next, and Vicki was amazing at this too, and we did end up with the polished sketches of what she had originally put down in the first few minutes in that initial meeting.

At the bottom of the bag she had drawn the silhouettes of the vegetable shoots in growth, subtly indicating the contents of the packet, as well as giving a natural out-of-the-ground feel.

We had briefed Vicki on the route to market we had identified as our given path for sales. We would start with independent farm shops, delis and food halls etc. Our plan was to then try and win some prestige listings like the food halls Harrods, Fortnum & Mason etc. Then we aspired to list with Ocado, Waitrose and other larger retailers. With this brief in mind, to give the packaging a feel of luxury and quality she added a subtle pinstripe to the bag design.

The packaging was just as important to me as the logo and brand. I met with a packaging supplier whom I used to work for years ago (17 to be exact!). They were and still are one of the leading packaging manufacturers in the UK, Ultimate Packaging, www.ultimate-packaging.co.uk. The meeting was with one of my old bosses, to whom I explained what I wanted from the packaging, the feel, the impact etc.

We had varying options we could have chosen but elected to go with something not that common at the

Claire's Diamond

You don't always need the most expensive option to look the best; creativity over money can take you further.

time; I certainly hadn't seen any crisp companies with this. It was paper on the outside with the foil laminated to the inside. I was also very fastidious on the weight/thickness of what I wanted the bags to be. It didn't look this way, but the paper on foil option was a few pence per bag cheaper than the normal foil on foil option, so that certainly helped with the decision from a cashflow and bottom line margins point of view.

I wanted people who picked my packet of crisps up to be sold on them at that point. I wanted them to buy into what the brand and products stood for: healthier and premium. All the thought and toil which had gone into bringing this brand to life. Absolutely every minor detail had to be just right, and I believed we had all the right people and ingredients in place now to make this so: brand, logo, packaging, production.

We had our supply sorted albeit through the third party in Borehamwood and had been in contact with the factory in the Netherlands. We had confirmation of their BRC Grade A production status. (When you wish to trade with the retailers, they will need you to have production accreditation of either SALSA or BRC.) So the next step was to get the packaging printed so we could get our hands on some crisps to sell.

I worked closely with Ultimate Packaging on all the finer detail as the packaging went into production. This included being at the print press to approve as the packaging was coming off the line. I'm sure I was one of their most picky customers, who was most probably spending the least amount of money in comparison to their business size. This initial packaging production accounted for 15% of my loan funding though, so to me it was huge.

Next stop Holland. John and I went over on a ferry to witness the first production run of crisps. On the ferry going over I recall us sitting in the bar area on the top deck where there was a piano playing. We were excited to get to the factory, talking about Scrubbys, and we made a list of what we wanted to achieve with the brand. Our 'mission statement' almost. It was along these lines:

- Exceed all expectations.
- Be that good the buyers come to us.
- Try to achieve a royal warrant (this had been sparked in me when I was in the London food halls researching way back when).

The day had arrived for us to see the production happening. The factory was huge. I had not been in very many food factories at all. I'd visited a few back in my packaging selling days, but not many at all, and certainly nothing like this one.

We were instructed to put all the correct factory clothing on: hairnets, shoe covers, jackets, and wash our hands etc. Once in there we saw the full process from the mud-coated vegetables in crates, right through to the finished crisps coming down the conveyor belt to the packing line.

It was here my heart sank. Now although I hadn't been in very many factories at all, and certainly never seen a full cycle of food production like this, I knew something was wrong. At the line end where the packs were being sealed ready to go into the boxes, lots of them were being rejected and dropping off the line.

I asked the production manager who was showing us round what was wrong. Why weren't the bags sealing?

In terms of the crisps, the production method, the USPs etc., one of the attributes or 'characters' was that due to the cooking process being at a lower temperature, the raw slices of vegetable once cooked didn't disintegrate, and reduce down to what 'normal' vegetable crisps do. I am sure we are all familiar with them; they look like potpourri.

Anyway, given that the vegetables retained their large slices, this meant that if a large slice of carrot, for instance, dropped into the bag last ready to be sealed (the bags kept on being filled until the electronic weight checker signalled they were at the desired weight; in this instance it was the 40g bags) it would stop the bag sealing at the top.

This was happening very frequently; all the vegetables were in large slices. You can imagine how large some of the parsnip and sweet potato slices were too. These made for a good 'dipping' tool, which we later used in our marketing communications, but more on that later. Right here and now we had a production problem.

I asked for the production line to be stopped, and on closer examination it looked as though there was a problem with the packaging. Hours later we got to the bottom of this: the factory had sent us the wrong cutter guide for the packaging. This was a disaster.

When you originate packaging, you have along with the actual rolls of packaging film what are called 'plates'. These are the templates for future packaging

Claire's Diamond

Always speak up. Never ever ever keep your mouth shut when you know something is wrong.

to be run on, and cost, in our case, circa £1200 for each set (we had a set for the 40g and a set for the 100g).

The bottom line was that 50,000 impressions (that was the minimum print run), and the plates for the 40g bags, were a write-off. The consequences of this for us were:

- We would have to battle with the factory to pay for the plates and packaging as it was their error. We had the added layer of complication of going through Borehamwood.
- We would have to launch with just the one bag of crisps – this meant just selling the 100g bags, which really reduced the places we could approach and our planned route to market from the off.

We couldn't delay our launch as I had already left my employment. We needed to start trading ASAP.

We left the factory with this realisation. At the platform on the train station in Holland waiting for our train I felt so deflated, I sat on a bench and just cried. I was worried. My instinct told me that this wasn't going to be a quick thing to get sorted.

The battle over the packaging and consequences would have to wait its turn in our list of priorities, and right now we had to deal with the matter in hand: launching with what we did have.

Claire's Diamond

It's no good waiting until you have this and that; if you wait you'll never get off the blocks. Start now, start today with what you do have, otherwise you'll wait forever.

The Practical Stuff

Great stuff, you're making progress now. Here's what comes next: steps 3 and 4.

STEP 3:
Product Creation, Testing Your Product and Market

Will you make your product yourself?

As I've said before, a lot of food businesses start with production in their own kitchens in their home. There's absolutely nothing wrong in that, and it is a very good low-cost way to play around with flavours, ingredients etc.

At this stage it is worth giving thought to where you see your product being sold. Are you aiming at the retailers, if so would you be able to cope with high volumes if you remained producing from your kitchen? Refer to your business plan. You should find the answer to your question in there.

Is the aim of your business to retail at markets and small artisan delis and farm shops? Is the product you are launching able to be produced at home, or do you need to outsource due to a specialist production method? As with the initial grass roots product research, the same needs to be done with regards to the production.

Make some samples

Once you have decided on your prototype, you need to find some guinea pigs, some honest taste testers! Make some samples (or get some made) and ask family and friends for their HONEST opinion.

Beware of the 'ugly baby' here though. Friends or family members aren't always the best at being honest. This is one reason why I always maintain my opinion of trading on a market stall is the best way to start out with your product – you don't have anywhere to hide when there is just 4ft of wood between you and your customer.

Ask for feedback on all aspects: taste, flavour, texture, smell, ingredients etc. These are all the attributes your product will be tested on when you do launch and are entering awards (which I strongly suggest you do). We won multiple awards for Scrubbys, and the impact on sales and brand awareness is not to be underestimated.

Tell them what you expect your RRP (recommended retail price) to be; would they happily pay that? They must be totally truthful with you, as you have a lot riding on this – sometimes all your life savings, so there's no time for being nice so as not to upset you or hurt your feelings! You could also run a focus group – all of this will be valuable research later down the line too when talking to food buyers.

Taste scrumptious

Focus on making your products and brand exceptional. Your product must taste DELICIOUS. It's not good enough to have all the correct commercials, nutritionals,

Claire's Diamond

Don't worry about being first to market – concentrate on quality and getting it right. If your idea, product and brand stand up, they always will whether you are first or not.

market data etc. etc. in place if your product doesn't pass the taste test.

Even impressive packaging and a killer marketing campaign won't work if your product will only be bought once! So, no matter how long it takes, or how much you're itching to get your product out there, do not compromise on this!

As you have read in the opening chapters, the whole reason I wanted to create my product and brand was to bring a healthier option to market. Although some of the methods would have given me an even lower fat and calorie product, it's no good hitting the health credentials if the taste isn't there.

STEP 4:
Mandatory Labelling, Legislation and Legals

Is your product ambient, chilled or frozen?

These are the three main categories your product will fit into. From this you will be able to determine the shelf life anyone retailing your product will expect, and what shelf life you need to work to if you're not already there. It will also be hugely important from a logistics point of view: how you get your product delivered to your customers, and also the costs associated.

With Scrubbys we had a very low-cost and slick logistics operation. In part it was driven by the knowledge that we had to be sure we kept these costs down as we had quite large (and to a degree unpredictable) manufacturing costs due to buying in Euros. We rented contract storage where the pallets of crisps were delivered to, and from there the cases of crisps were either distributed on the pallet network or dispatched via a delivery company.

There are many to choose from, but we found www.directexpresslogistics.co.uk very good. If we had larger orders (pallets) they went straight on the pallet network which our contract storage company, www.easttrans.co.uk, took care of; again there are many out there, but be sure to use a provider who has food grade storage.

You will need to know all of these to work out your costs of goods (COGS) later through the process.

AMBIENT – These are food types which can be stored at room temperature.

CHILLED – These are food types which will be sold from a refrigerator.

FROZEN – These are food types which will be sold from freezers.

Shelf life testing

This is a compulsory legal requirement. You must go through this process; you cannot sell food or drink without it. It's part of being ready to retail your product. There are plenty of shelf life testing providers who you can work with to get this done. You can also have accelerated shelf life testing carried out if you don't want to or don't have the time to wait the full amount of 'real time' i.e. 12-month ambient shelf life testing, when you don't have the year to wait.

If you are outsourcing production, the manufacturer you are working with will have all this information already, which will make life easier on this front.

Food labelling

Allergen labelling, mandatory food information and nutrition labelling are all things which you need to have an understanding of. Food Information Regulations (FIR) are reviewed on a regular basis so this is an ongoing area to keep up to date with. Your product will need to be applicably labelled before you sell any.

As with the shelf life testing, if you have a third party manufacturer they may be able to help with this, but the liability of the product falls with you as the brand owner. You are the customer of the manufacturer, but your customers are just that: yours. They are not the customer of your manufacturer, so you have the liability.

If you are planning on your products being suitable and accredited for vegetarians, vegans, or coeliacs, now would be a good time to look into all their requirements at this stage too. You can find more information on these here:

http://www.vegsocapproved.com/info

https://www.vegansociety.com/your-business/are-you-registered

https://www.coeliac.org.uk/
food-industry-professionals/
the-crossed-grain-symbol/

You may also wish to explore Fairtrade or Organic accreditation; more information can be found here:

https://www.fairtrade.org.uk/For-Business

https://www.soilassociation.org/

Register as a food business

You must contact your local authority and register as a food business. This is required no matter whether you produce your product yourself or outsource your production. If you haven't also done so already you need to incorporate your trading business with Companies House.

It is worth noting that your trading/brand name doesn't have to be the same name you register at Companies House. E.g. your brand might be 'Pinkies', but your registered company name at Companies House might be Pinkies Foods Limited, or something completely different to that.

In terms of the trademark for your brand, take care of where this sits, i.e. will you personally own it or will your business own the mark? If you are hoping to bring investors into your business in the future, the mark will most probably be an asset of the business, as opposed to you personally owning the mark. I am no lawyer or accountant, but it may also be worth talking to either/

both of these if you own the mark first and transfer it to your business if there is a benefit/negative to this.

Packaging

All the above will need to be in place BEFORE you have your packaging designed or printed. Doing all the above first and including it on your packaging from the off will help prevent costly mistakes in both time and money aspects. As I mentioned about the plates being originated, all this detail will go on your plates. Any changes you wish to make going forward to your packaging could mean a full set of plates, so I can't stress enough making sure you have it all in place before you sign off any packaging.

Insurance

You will need the necessary insurances in place before you launch; this will vary depending on your route to market, i.e. direct retail or multiples. When you are successful in securing a listing with the retailers they will typically ask that you have public liability in place of £2million. Even if you are just trading on a market stall or smaller independents, you still need insurance in place.

Food safety and hygiene

Take a food safety and hygiene course; these are easily accessible and you will need to do this even if you only attend markets and festivals with your product; the event organisers will want proof that you hold this certification. These can also be carried out online, via providers such as www.virtual-college.co.uk.

Real Account

HOW I'VE HELPED AND
WORKED WITH A FOOD BUSINESS

I'm Hayley Burdett, Founder and MD of Bay's Kitchen.

I began working on Bay's Kitchen in June 2016 and it took until April 2018 to launch!

I went through a huge rollercoaster ride with the development, made a few mistakes along the way, spent money where I shouldn't but finally made it to the point where I was launching!

The rollercoaster ride of development was very difficult at times, particularly as I was on my own, with no previous experience of the food industry.

I didn't have a co-founder to bounce ideas off, share the stress, work through problems, help with the decisions or share the work load. Whilst I made it through, I decided for the launch I needed some help. I wanted the launch to go smoothly and be a huge success and to avoid the huge pitfalls.

Due to my prior lack of knowledge of the food industry, I decided I could really do with some help at this stage, to ensure I had everything in line ready for approaching retailers and distributors.

Whilst I had an RRP and margins in mind and knew the retailers and distributors I wanted to approach, I really wanted to go through this with someone who had been there and done it, to make sure I got it right.

Claire had been recommended many times on The Food Hub group on Facebook, most recently by Charlotte Moore, who is a lovely lady! I knew if Charlotte recommended her, then Claire would be lovely too! I knew Claire had previously launched a brand of her own and was now working as a consultant, so I emailed her to ask for her help with getting my business strategy, planning and sales pitching right.

We first had a free half hour call, and I instantly knew I'd work really well with Claire, that she would really care about my business and that she would provide invaluable knowledge and support.

Claire then sent over an outline of what she could offer, along with her rates. I accepted and got to work compiling all the info I could to send to Claire for her to understand my business and be able to provide me with the strategy doc, presentation outline, contacts and more.

At the end of her day's work she sent everything over and I couldn't have been happier! True value for money. I really felt ready to start approaching the retailers and distributors. Since then I have worked with Claire again on understanding promotional plans and I am sure we will be working together again soon, hopefully when I get to crunch time with new retailers!

Working with Claire is one of the best decisions I have made for my business. She has taught me a lot, has been there on email and calls and given me the confidence and tools to successfully launch my business, without hitting the major pitfalls which some businesses do at this stage.

Hayley Burdett | Founder, Bay's Kitchen
www.bayskitchen.co.uk

What Would Claire Do Now?

I'd launch with more than one product – looking back we were crazy to launch with just one bag of crisps. Some categories you would be able to launch with just one product, if it were a niche item, but we were targeting such a big category so the potential to get lost was huge.

Yes, we'd have had both the 40g and 100g if we hadn't had the packaging problem. Even so though, due to the limited knowledge I had of buyers at this time, the 40g and 100g were to sit in completely different areas.

Essentially, I had to try and convince a buyer to remove a range and replace their offering with one pack of crisps, and that was never going to happen. We most probably should have launched with two variants in the 100g bag size, and not tried to split our routes to market with a 40g and 100g. This could have given us more weight with the retailers initially as we'd have had two to offer.

Maybe I shouldn't have quit my day job as fast. I knew why I did, and in all honesty that's the kind of person I am – all in. So, to say I wouldn't do the same again is a lie. What I am saying though is that it made life so much harder; perhaps it didn't have to be. Who knows; we never will now.

Worrying about paying the mortgage and all the other bills, looking after the kids etc. along with the pressure of selling enough to keep the cashflow alive is not for the fainthearted. If there is a way to keep some money

Claire's Diamond

This is where you need to know yourself, really know yourself. Don't be swayed by the mass of people you will no doubt have around you right now.

coming in to cover your personal bases that's what I would advise. If you are in the position where you are launching with savings to cover you, be realistic on how long you can survive and what T/O (turnover) you need to achieve and when by.

If you are like me, though, and the same all-in character, then be prepared for the hardest thing you have ever done. It's not impossible; after all I did it. What it is, though, is all consuming. By this I mean be prepared to work seven days a week, 15-hour days at the very least; add kids into the mix and life will be a blur for about two years.

Only you know how you tick, what makes you tick. Do you thrive under pressure? Are you the kind of person who likes to have things more measurable and predictable? Find these answers and stick with them. There is no right or wrong way. Every single business founder/entrepreneur will have slightly different ways of working, what motivates them etc. Have belief in you and do what you know you can do.

Exercise:

What YOU should do now

Production – Will you produce yourself or look for a third-party manufacturer? List your options here.
Which category does your product fit into: Ambient, Chilled or Frozen, and how will you test shelf life? It's also worth looking into the logistics at this stage – how will you deliver your products?
What accreditations do you want prior to signing packaging off?

What kind of packaging will your product come in, and where will you get this from?
Insurance: make a list of potential providers.
Register as a food business and register your company at Companies House. Who is your local authority, and what is your company name?
Food Safety and Hygiene Course – make a list here of providers and costs.

CHAPTER 4

Buckle Up, You're About to Go Warp Speed

Our first delivery of crisps arrived and right there and then the penny dropped: how on earth were we going to sell all of these crisps?! One of the first things I did was contact our local press; they did a photo-shoot and interviewed us for a piece in the paper.

It's now May 2012, the 19th to be exact, and this was to be Scrubbys' official birthday. I wasn't expecting our news to make the entire front page complete with full colour picture, and a column inside too, but remember what I've shared about being a disruptive influence and not being a wall-flower, well I was starting as I was determined to carry on, and was going to have to get used to our picture being on the front page – throughout the journey it happened quite a few times.

On the same day, we were sampling in a local farm shop, www.unclehenrys.co.uk, without a doubt one of the best in the country. This was our first stockist, and we soon learned that supporting the listing with sampling (edible marketing) was a winner.

I remember the first pack of crisps going through the till. Stood with our youngest daughter, seeing 'Scrubbys' come up on the till and printed on the receipt, was a memory I won't ever forget. We had done it. We were officially launched and selling our crisps. It was the best feeling.

I had also learned that the local Chamber of Commerce had their annual awards dinner coming up, so I contacted the organiser with a request to pop a packet of crisps in the goodie bags. She agreed so I attached my business card to each packet and stuffed them in the goodie bags. This resulted in another local deli stocking Scrubbys.

Sales was the name of the game. We had to use every resource, every trick in the book we could to get the crisps out there. A trade show I knew of (through all the research I had previously done) was coming up. It's firmly on the calendar of great shows to exhibit at if you are in this region: www.gff.co.uk organised by The Guild of Fine Food. These are the same organisers of the Great Taste Awards (these are awards which you simply must enter) https://gff.co.uk/awards/great-taste-awards/ if your turnover is less than £1million. It's only £56 per product to enter.

The return you can reap from winning this is immense both in terms of increased credibility for your product and brand, but also in sales of the product when it proudly displays the Gold Star logo.

The show was at the Yorkshire Event Centre. It was to be the first trade show we'd done. We had attended plenty over the research years but had little idea of what to do from an exhibitor point of view.

We had all our marketing material, pop-up roller banners, leaflets, crisps, sampling bowls etc. All the usual paraphernalia. We'd opted for clear carrier bags to give samples away in rather than the expense of printed ones and let the actual bags of crisps in the carrier bags do the talking, and this worked a treat. Our packaging was so eye-catching you couldn't help but notice it.

At these shows you have the opportunity to be chosen as one of the 'editor's picks' where your product is proudly displayed as one of the best products of the show. I was thrilled when Scrubbys was chosen.

The lucky picks are also awarded a certificate to proudly display on their stand. I am convinced this assisted in us bagging (no pun intended!), there and then at the show, a FULL PALLET order to a department store in Ireland – wow, I couldn't believe our luck. From there our day just kept on getting better.

As I was taking some time out walking around the show, chatting with other exhibitors, I heard of a 'feed the dragons panel' which was taking place later that afternoon. On the panel there were some buyers from various places ranging from distributors to local farm shops and Harrods. I just knew we had to pitch. I found out who to speak to and asked if they could squeeze us in.

Bingo – we were accepted. I thought if we could get a listing with a distributor, which in this case was Cotswold Fayre, we would really be on our way and gaining some sales traction. The pitch session came; John was the one doing the pitching. It went like a dream; Cotswold Fayre expressed an interest and an appointment was made for us to go and meet with them.

This was amazing. We were just seven weeks old as a brand, and were rocking and rolling. The meeting with Cotswold went well, they listed us and we were to be included in their next catalogue. I was still wracking my brains for ways to get out there more, raise brand awareness, and most importantly keep the sales coming in.

One morning listening to Radio 2 I heard Chris Evans announce a new festival he was the brainchild of, Carfest, and they were on the lookout for 'Britain's Best' food producers to trade at the festival.

That's it, I thought – that was where we needed to be. There was a strict application process where you had to submit details of your product, your brand and why you believed you were Britain's Best.

I completed the application, crossed my fingers and submitted it. We were successful in being accepted, not for just one of the festivals but BOTH, WOW! There was to be a Carfest North and a Carfest South. I was over the moon. I thought presence at this festival would firmly put us on the map. Little did I realise just how big these festivals would come to be for us.

The events information pack came. The first festival, South, was to be at Laverstoke Park in August. The North was a couple of weeks later at Cholmondeley Castle. I could tell these had fun written all over them; the kids would love them, we could sell a ton of crisps, and hopefully pick up some more stockists.

I put a plan into action of how best to fully 'work' the show. I decided to get us some balloons printed to give to kids at the festival. We also had some polo shirts printed with Scrubbys on, not just for John and me but for our kids too. We also decided to make the most of the stand from a height aspect by having some bunting made with our branding on. We arrived en masse and believe me, there was no way of escaping Scrubbys!

Just in the same way as I'd invented a mission for myself to meet Peter Jones at the MADE Festival, I had thrown the gauntlet down to myself once more and decided that I was going to try and get in front of Chris Evans, somehow get Scrubbys on his radar.

So, my 'meet Chris Evans' mission began. When we arrived on site I had a good hunt around, to find where the VIP and glamping areas were; my plan was to give them some crisps. Thought process being, if the crisps were in there, there would be a chance that he would eat some.

That hunt was successful; I found the relevant areas and asked if they would like some crisps, which they accepted. The first full trading day of the festival arrived. We were all in the marquee, with the Scrubbys stand set up to perfection. I had seen Chris come in to the Britain's Best tent, and word amongst the traders was that he would come back in the following morning.

They were long days at the show, trading from the stand for 10 hours. The kids did so well, especially George. He'd only just turned eight years old. We kept them occupied by enlisting them to hand the balloons out to every child they could find. This worked; I recall Lucy coming back to the stand after watching one of the live singers and saying all she could see from the back of the crowd were people waving their Scrubbys balloons: a perfect example of guerrilla marketing in action.

George quickly learned how to charm the other traders into doing swapsies: a bag of Scrubbys for a chocolate car or pouch of olives! I remember him proudly coming back to the stand one time with the wares he'd traded for, declaring 'That's how you do business!' Remember what I said about what we teach our kids without even knowing we are – I feel sure some of these experiences will go on to positively shape the kids in later life.

Abigail turned into a saleswoman at these festivals, proudly reciting the sales pitch perfectly to everyone who stopped by the stand.

Sunday, the last day, was here, and I was determined to meet Chris. We'd done all we could and were without doubt getting noticed. We knew this because practically everyone who came to the stand commented that they'd seen one of the kids in their Scrubbys t-shirts or had seen balloons around the festival, and they'd come to find out where and who Scrubbys were.

We'd organised our stand differently to the other traders. Most had their 6ft trestle table straight in front of them, but from all my experience on market stalls, etc., I knew this wasn't always the best way as it creates a barrier, plus you can't 'invite' people into your stand; there's no room.

We had our table running the other way and by doing so this gave us a little area within our space for people to come into our stand. This turned out to be perfect for Chris to come and sit on our stand and talk to us for a good 10 minutes.

He came into the marquee, and I could see him right over the other side. He was making his way around the traders; we were to be the last he came to, and to my amazement he sat down and chatted with the kids. He complimented us on the fact that we were everywhere; I recall he said, 'Well done; you're everywhere... you're in my tent and at the bar'. He'd seen the kids, the balloons, and loved the crisps. He sat there chatting, signed the kids' t-shirts and the crowd had gathered around our stand. It was packed.

I then went in for the kill: 'Chris, can we have a photo of you with our crisps, or don't you do that?' His response was to pick the packet of Scrubbys from our hands, whack it in his mouth and put his arms around me and John, boom... we had the money shot! I was gobsmacked. This was even better than I had dared to imagine.

Claire's Diamond

Whatever you do, do it with all you've got. Passion is contagious.

The whole festival was a resounding success, and we couldn't wait for the next one in a couple of weeks at Cholmondeley Castle. When we arrived home, I got in touch with our local newspaper (again) to share our Chris Evans meeting shenanigans. I wasn't expecting to be front page colour once more. Crikey, here we were, fresh off the starting blocks, just 12 weeks old and we were front page again with an endorsement of how amazing our crisps were from the nation's No.1 DJ.

We went on to do both Carfests every year. Some of our most precious memories from the Scrubbys journey with the kids are from Carfest. I met some lovely people there who have now become friends, not least one lady called June.

A few times we'd managed to get ourselves staying in the glamping area of the festival. I don't mind admitting we stuck out like sore thumbs. I won't forget some of the looks I got one morning, going into the breakfast tent in our onesies, and me with my hair in rollers.

It was the easiest way to get my hair out of my face to crack on with getting the kids sorted and all that was needed for the stand, etc. Anyway, there was an area

Claire's Diamond

Have the courage to embrace who you truly are. Don't shrink or try and change; be yourself... always.

with electricity for ladies to do their hair and makeup etc. I'm in the tent drying my daughter's hair (in my rollers), when this lady commented on them: 'They're fab, did you do them yourself?'

She was impressed that they were so orderly and what a great idea they were. We had a full-on conversation about all sorts. At first, I felt a bit out of my depth because she was a VIP (one of Chris's friends), and I was in a onesie and rollers, but then the conversation went on, and we met her again at the coming festivals, and are now firm friends.

We had such a laugh with the kids camping and glamping. Meeting numerous celebrities, watching all the bands and air shows. All whilst we were growing our brand and selling crisps. What was not to like?

How were we going to keep that momentum though?

The Practical Stuff

We are now gaining good pace, and some of the fun stuff starts now: step 5.

STEP 5:
Creating and Bringing Your Brand to Life

There are various elements to creating your brand:

NAME – What are you calling your brand?

LOGO – What is the identity going to look like?

PERSONALITY – What personality will your brand have?

VALUES – What will your brand say, what values will it have, and what meaning will consumers take from it?

Your product is what you will sell; your brand is what holds your product. Think about what you want your brand identity to be; what is your brand character, and how will you communicate this? You must be consistent across all channels: your name, your packaging, your social media etc.

Name

Think about your brand name, check that this is available, and that the relevant social media handles are available also. Will you face any trademark oppositions? Learn from my experience on this one. Try, if you can, to think forward. If you were to extend your range, or move into complementary categories, will the name you are thinking of stretch out?

Logo

You may have a logo idea in mind. Think about what colours you want to use, and how will you make your logo memorable and stand out. Be mindful that when your product sits on the shelf, be that in large retail or in a small farm shop/deli, it needs to catch the consumer's eye in a second.

You could have a 'mock-up' of this made and run a focus group, just like with the taste test. Don't be afraid to ask for others' opinions; it's so easy to become blinkered. You'll be living with your name and logo for a long time, so investing time and effort into this will be invaluable.

Personality

What will your brand personality be: young, old, cheeky, funny, healthy, loud etc.? The personality of your brand can be transferred into your brand name and logo style, so give a full brief including the personality you want running through your brand when you speak to designers.

Values

Who is your customer? How old are they? Are they gender specific? These questions and more are all important to ask yourself when you are pulling all the above together and will all help you.

Brand

It's worth taking some time to look at other successful brands you like and admire: who are they, and why do you like them; what aspect of their brand draws you? What personality do they have, and how do they successfully convey this?

Using the research you already have into the category in which your product will sit, and your competitors, you will have an idea on what you need to do to stand out amongst them.

A brand is not a logo. Your brand is the story that you tell about your business in all your communications. It is more than a colour scheme or a font. Your brand is the promise of what your customers will get by purchasing your brand: your values and your beliefs.

Real Account

HOW I'VE HELPED AND WORKED WITH A FOOD BUSINESS

I got in touch with Claire while looking for help with my business, Nom Foods – an organic and free-from snack company.

At the time, the business was a couple of years old and having started it on my own (and being stretched pretty thin!) I really wanted some guidance. I was feeling the isolation that running a business on your own can bring, and so caught up in the day to day jobs that I wasn't taking a step back, looking at the bigger picture and creating a strategy for growth.

I was feeling the pressure of being in a competitive market without the huge new product development and marketing budgets that are often needed to substantially grow a brand. In one day, Claire looked at everything from sales figures to marketing plans and advised on how best to achieve the growth we needed to reach the next level working with the resources and strengths that we had.

One of the main things Claire offered Nom was an experienced pair of eyes looking over sales strategy and giving sound advice about how to make goals and achieve them.

The fact that Claire has been there before with her own brand gives her an authenticity and understanding that can sometimes be lacking from speakers or consultants who haven't had hands-on experience with running their own brand.

Claire's friendliness, energy and enthusiasm really gave me confidence and a refreshed energy to push forward and since then, the business has grown considerably, won awards, gained supermarket listings, launched new products, and so much more!

Steph Croft-Simon | Founder, Nom Foods
www.nomfoods.co.uk

What Would Claire Do Now?

Our brand was something which we 100% got right. We were awarded CoolBrands status for Scrubbys in both 2013/14 and 2016/17. The name divided opinion sometimes, but I am of the thought that if you can get people engaged and talking about your brand then you're onto a winner.

As I have explained we invented the Scrubbys name in a matter of hours, but this isn't an ideal way to get there, and I would always recommend taking time over naming your brand. Budget depending you can work with some amazing branding companies, however there is nothing to suggest that like me you can't get there in your own way.

There will always be a mass of people around you on this journey willing to put their hand in your pocket. You can, before you know it, burn through a lot of cash. Be mindful of this. Ask yourself if it is really needed each time before you are thinking of spending any money.

Claire's Diamond

When all logic and practicality says no, but your gut and instinct won't let it go, then you know you must do it.

Claire's Diamond

Hold on to your equity for as long as you can. You will require funding throughout your journey, so don't sell yourself short at start-up stage.

Business/Brand Name Worksheet

Once you've done your big brain dump, narrow it down and list 3 name ideas for your brand.

1.

2.

3.

List 3 brands/competitors currently in your space.

1.

2.

3.

List words you can associate with your:

Product:

Production method:

Ingredients:

Your name:

The function of your product:

Once you have got all of the above down…

- Have a look at how you can merge words, e.g. 'Scrub & Brumby' = Scrubbys.

- Say it out loud – how does it sound?

- Check if all the social media handles you'll need are available.

- Check out if trademarks are available.

- Run it past family and friends.

Exercise:

What YOU should do now

Name – Here's where you can do a brain dump of all the potential brand names you can think of. There will literally be loads, and over time you'll narrow them down to a few/couple.

Logo – You may have an idea in mind of what you want your logo to look like, what colours etc. Pop your thoughts down here.

Jot down the 'character' and personality of your brand. Make sure it will resonate with the target consumer you have identified.

What are your brand values; what do you want your brand to stand for?

Other brands you admire, and why – pop these down. Identify what they do which makes you admire them.

CHAPTER 5

Igniting the Market, and Being a Disruptive Guerrilla

We'd come off the starting blocks at amazing speed and there was no letting up. We'd decided to introduce another flavour and start expanding our range. We carried out some research and worked with the factory on some NPD (New Product Development) trials.

We suspected our third party in Borehamwood intercepted the samples from the factory and pitched them to Sainsbury's for their own label – we couldn't prove it, but that's something you need to try and safeguard against should you find yourself in the same situation.

Ideally don't go through a third party, but we had no choice, no choice whatsoever. This made for so many complications, not least the added layer of cost. When you're dealing in such tight margins, that extra 5% off the bottom line makes things very hard indeed.

They weren't successful, however this delayed us. We eventually nailed the flavour profile, and all our trials tasted amazing. During the time since we'd launched, quite accidentally we'd built up a strong following of consumers choosing Scrubbys for the gluten-free aspect.

The original line (four vegetable mix: beetroot, carrot, parsnip and carrot) flavoured with sea salt was naturally gluten-free, but we wanted to launch a flavoured crisp, and remain gluten-free. These were to be parsnip crisps with chilli & lime flavour – at the time this went on to be the only flavoured gluten-free vegetable crisp available.

Even this didn't happen without its challenges. We'd run trials which had gone perfectly, but when it came to the final production run, for some reason the flavouring wasn't sticking to the parsnips. I will never forget the delivery arriving (I was due to leave that day for a trade mission to Iceland).

I went to our contract storage, as I did with every single delivery that came in, to quality check. I would check not only the crisps, but the boxes for any damage, and the packaging to make sure the cutter on the packaging film had cut off in the correct place. On occasion when it hadn't the bag design wasn't right, and this devalued the brand.

As I have shared previously, the detail is something which you can never overlook. With anything there is a right and a wrong. In our case if there was anything wrong with the crisps, the packaging or the way the delivery had arrived I would flag it up immediately with the factory and rectify it.

Claire's Diamond

One degree away here and there from what is right, and you end up with something too far from what you are, what you stand for and what your consumers expect. Attention to detail is paramount; you can't dilute this.

I opened some bags of crisps, and inside were the most delicious parsnips, but just as I'd experienced on this rollercoaster before for varying reasons, my heart sank. The flavouring was not on any of the crisps. It was sitting in the bottom of the bag. I cancelled my Iceland trip and went straight to Holland.

After a lot of time, effort and money we got the problem sorted by reformulating the flavouring. At one point it was strongly suggested that we needed to ditch our gluten-free aspirations, but I knew this was something which was right for our brand and consumers, so I fought hard on this and stuck to my guns. One of our first stockists for the parsnip with chilli & lime was Harrods.

I remember sampling in Harrods; it was a surreal moment. Years earlier I'd been in the food hall researching products to sell on our market stall, collating ideas on what product to launch, and there I was now stood with my brand, my product. It was crazy.

This was one of those moments where I had to pinch myself to check it was real. The highs and lows were starting to come at alarming speed; one minute something amazing like this would happen, the next we'd be faced with something that at the time seemed unsurmountable like the flavouring or packaging problems.

The conversation I'd had back at the MADE Festival with Wilfred Emmanuel-Jones and his advice, 'be a disruptive influence', was never far from my mind every single day. Any time I was flagging, or the challenges were coming thick and fast, I would recite this.

Claire's Diamond

Hold your dream and vision; if you want it badly enough and work hard enough it will come good.

One of the biggest challenges any new business faces, food or otherwise, is staying alive in the early days. Having enough sales coming in so you're not starved of cashflow. If you don't have sales you die; it's fundamentally as simple as that. This was our challenge: keeping sales flowing and raising brand awareness to convert consumers to Scrubbys.

I carried out all the sales and marketing activity myself for Scrubbys, not least because we couldn't afford to outsource this. The resources I used in the main were all forms of social media and my good friend guerrilla marketing. How lucky are we that we have these tools at our disposal?

I remember back in my double glazing and packaging sales days having to solely rely on the good old yellow pages, a road map and cold calling using good ole shoe leather!

Part of my marketing activity was a competition on our website, 'The Great British Dip Competition'.

This was for multiple reasons:

- It helped us to communicate a USP of our crisps: due to the crisps being so large, they were a perfect dipping tool.
- The above gave us an additional eating occasion to promote to our consumers, so we were more than just a packet of crisps.
- We were able to gauge where taste buds were heading, a form of market research.
- It gave us a 'hook' to interact with people.

- It helped build our list and following in general.
- All of the above was good activity to build into our retailer pitches further down the line.

Twitter was fast becoming the standout resource for me. I'd heard of the competition Theo Paphitis (a former Dragon) runs to be part of his #SBS club and decided to give it a shot. #SBS stands for Small Business Sunday and was started by Theo Paphitis in October 2010 when word has it he was feeling a bit bored after a Sunday lunch.

Theo was constantly being 'pitched to' and he wanted to help small businesses, so he set up a time and place to do that. It's on Sunday evenings from 5–7.30pm. The winners are chosen each Monday and Theo sends a tweet to his now 506,000 followers at 8pm to announce the six winners that week. Twitter goes crazy. There have now been 329,000 applications since it started in 2010.

Yes, you guessed it, after a few attempts at tweeting Theo, on the 10th February 2013 we learned that we had won! My tweet went along the lines of *'Scrubbys vegetable crisps which taste amazing. Family business working hard and loving it. Love to win #SBS'*.

I remember the Monday night; my phone suddenly went crazy as we gained loads of new followers on Twitter and picked up new stockists. That week I issued a press release which got us featured in press and on local radio shows. All of this going on and we were still less than a year old.

Claire's Diamond

Like attracts like; good attracts good. When you are in that flow, go with it, keep in it, hang out with like minded people, find your tribe.

During the first year we traded at a food festival or market literally every weekend. We toured the country up and down. Often this saw us attending dual events with the kids in tow; John would be at one event with one or two of the kids and I would be at another with the other one or two.

They got quite used to making the van into a mobile tent, padding it out with their sleeping bags in the early hours whilst putting up with being trailed here, there and everywhere on yet another 'Scrubbys Adventure'!

We entered awards, won some, and got shortlisted for others. We were featured in top newspapers like the *Independent*, *Telegraph*, *Daily Mail* and *Metro*. We entered and were shortlisted for business awards.

Remember the Chamber awards where I got Scrubbys into the goodie bags? Well I entered us in them the following year. The awards were two days before our first birthday. We were runners up in two categories: New Business Award, and Innovation Award. I'm sure you'll agree, what a fabulous year!

Just where had all of this positive disruptive guerrilla action in our first year in business taken us?

Not bad, eh, I'm sure you'll agree – but there was still so much more to do and achieve.

Our cashflow wasn't the healthiest and we desperately needed to grow beyond the stockists we'd got listings with. We had a good coverage of stockists through the network of independents and distributors we had but needed more sales.

Some good examples of us deploying shameless guerrilla tactics found us on local TV.

For those of you who may not be familiar with the marketing activity which is referred to as guerrilla, it's an activity you enter into in an unconventional way with little/no money to spend. It requires high energy and imagination, with the desired outcome being to grasp the attention of the public in a more personal and memorable way.

We'd heard through a friend that the local TV station was going to a shop in town near us. I enquired as to when the crew would be there, and John and I decided between us the best way to attack it so as not to look 'too obvious' so we didn't run the risk of not getting on TV.

We decided that it would look more believable, less 'staged', if just one of us was wearing our Scrubbys polo shirts. It worked; we were interviewed with John stood there all proudly logoed up, and it was aired later that night on the local news channels. Once again, these images found their way onto social media, all the while creating interest and momentum for the brand and gaining us farm shop or deli listings.

I won't ever forget my first 'proper' speaking gig as a positive outcome of effective use of guerrilla marketing. It was at the Baths Hall in Scunthorpe (I was born in Scunthorpe so that felt weird). I was one of the 'warm-up' speakers at an entrepreneurial conference for Dave Fishwick 'Bank of Dave'.

I was really nervous but he was so kind and helpful, just as Tim Campbell and Wilfred Emmanuel-Jones had been previously. I told him I was, and he just advised me to take lots of deep breaths backstage before I went on and guaranteed me that once I came off stage I'd be buzzing and wanting to do it again! He wasn't wrong; from that moment on I had the speaking bug!

Whilst I was trying to calm my nerves prior to going on to speak, I'd had a look round the room to gauge where the cameras were, what angles they were shooting from, and managed to place my Scrubbys pop-up roller banner in just the right place. For the entire conference whilst the TV and press cameras were on Dave Fishwick, the Scrubbys banner was there loud and proud in the background. Once again, we reaped rewards from this activity.

By this time, I felt confident enough to approach the next tier of customers we had on our hit list. These were Ocado and Waitrose. I think one of the most ballsy instances we had of unleashing our 'disruptive guerrilla tactics' was at a Carfest festival.

I'd been trying to get listings with both Ocado and Waitrose, and as is usually the case, it was taking an age to get anywhere with them. Both had expressed that they liked/were interested in Scrubbys but taking it further and nailing a listing was proving impossible.

I'd resorted to almost stalking the buyers. I'd email them early morning and late afternoon when I thought they might be at their desk, hoping to grab them when the hustle and bustle of the day wasn't hitting them. I did the same with phone calls; I tried every conceivable pattern you could imagine.

I'll never forget the toil of a couple of the early listings with Partridges and Fortnum & Mason. The reason Partridges was on my target list was down to my royal warrant aspirations.

I have no idea if it works this way at all, but my logic was that if Scrubbys were stocked somewhere which supplied the royal household that would be a good place to start. I'll share more on how royal connections and St James's Palace played a part in this adventure later.

It was a really hot day in August when I went to London with the sole aim of getting more traction with Partridges and Fortnum's. Duke of York Square was my first port of call. Armed with my double glazing approach to sales I determinedly strode into Partridges, naively thinking that you could just rock up to these places and have a chat with the buyer – oh how little did I know. You can't simply do this, as I swiftly found out when I was asked to leave the shop!

The air was blue with profanities as I called John and explained what had happened. Right there and then in my head I concluded that I WOULD turn this embarrassment into a listing with them. I did; it took a long time and a lot of relationship building with the buyer. This was more than worth it, as you'll find out later.

Fortnum & Mason brought out the 'stalker' in me once again. This was another store I knew we had to list with. It wasn't for volume of sales. These are what I now know are referred to as 'prestige' or 'flagship' listings, as they are good for your brand in terms of profile. I was knocked back numerous times by the buyer. I was having none of it though. I returned to the store time after time.

The final conversation and action which threw it my way was when I recounted to her via email a conversation I'd overheard two ladies having in the food area, expressing their disappointment at the lack of a dedicated gluten-free area.

In addition, I put together a show-stopping hamper of Scrubbys and left it in the staff entrance for the buyer to ensure she personally received it. And I added a note at the bottom of my email reading, 'I am aware I am becoming very persistent, but if I am to the point of becoming a pest, please tell me to go away'. Not long after this I got the listing.

Sampling in both Fortnum's and Partridges gave me the same high feeling that I'd had in Harrods. Scrubbys was my baby; I lived, breathed, ate and slept it.

At events/festivals if I'd have had £1 for everyone who wanted to know the nearest stockist of Scrubbys to them I'd have been very rich indeed! But money and time was running out for us, and we needed to get sales higher.

Part of our stand set-up at any festival or market we traded at was a blackboard on which we chalked the details about Scrubbys – lower fat, lower calories, price, and offers etc.

On one particular occasion at Carfest, fuelled by exasperation and my guerrilla marketing passion, I decided to wipe the board down and replace it with a plea asking the general public to tweet and in general be a bother to Ocado and Waitrose in the hope of getting them to stock Scrubbys. I will never know to what degree it actually impacted. However, I don't think it's a coincidence that in the coming weeks, conversations with both accelerated at a speed which we'd not had previously.

My situation was I didn't have anything to lose. Our cashflow situation was critical, which had led me to start looking for a job I could do alongside running Scrubbys. I applied for various jobs in food sales.

My thought process was, if I could get a job selling a product to the same type of customer I had for Scrubbys it would be a win-win situation. I could transfer some

Claire's Diamond

What have you got to lose? I always ask myself this is any given situation. Don't let fear hold you back, if you feel it... do it, and if you feel fear do it anyway.

of my customer base to whom I would work for, and hopefully convert some customers over to Scrubbys.

At the same time as looking for a job, I'd started to look for investment too. I reached out to my network which by this time was growing strong; through all the noise (positively disruptive) I had created I was starting to become less of an outsider in the industry.

Keeping up my inherent desire to network, learn and grow for the good of building Scrubbys, I heard of an event in Hull, another 'mock Dragon' panel. I applied for us to pitch, and we were accepted.

From that panel we met another amazing contact who became a friend (it turns out we are both keen open water swimmers) who helped in so many ways: Julian Wild, a solicitor and partner at a leading law firm, www.rollits.com. With 30 years' experience of buying and selling companies, mainly in the food and drink industry, you can imagine that Julian is very well connected.

We met at his offices a few weeks after that pitch, and explained where we were at and that we were looking for some investment. Through some of his connections we were fortunate enough to get some investment in return for a small equity sale. This was the lifeline that we needed.

It was a stepping stone, to keep the wolf from the door. It only gave us some brief respite, though, and the need for bigger investment was becoming clearer by the day.

One afternoon, whilst doing some book-keeping, I got distracted, as I am sure most of us do when faced with necessary but not the most exciting tasks! This distraction took me to Twitter. I was trawling through Scrubbys' feed, and saw a tweet mentioning *Dragons' Den*, with details of how to pitch to the Dragons.

I completed the application on their website, and received a reply saying should they be interested they'd get in touch. It was only about an hour or so and my phone rang; a researcher for *Dragons' Den*, Fran, was on the phone...!

The Practical Stuff

Here's some nitty gritty to get stuck into. All the steps are important, but here's one to really understand and spend a lot of time on: step 6. Then you're ready for step 7 which is the sales and marketing of your product.

STEP 6:
Sales and Pricing

Costs (COGS – Cost of Goods Sold)

You must be totally inside all your production costs, and need to include everything from the raw ingredients, production, right down to delivering your product to its end destination. If you do not know your costs thoroughly this will have repercussions further down the line on all your margins and will of course affect your profits.

You also need to have a very clear understanding of these to know where any savings can be made as you scale and grow; for instance, ingredient, manufacture or distribution savings.

There will be different costs associated with each revenue stream you have. For example, delivery costs in my instance via APC to smaller stockists were different to deliveries via the pallet network to retailers.

In terms of product too, costs of goods may vary. In my case I was able to gain a competitive edge to help me target different markets by reducing the bag size from 100g to 90g with a three-vegetable mix as opposed to four vegetables. Clearly the cost of goods in this pack was different.

It's essential to drill these down right to the last penny per unit. These costs make a critical impact on your bottom line, and as you grow and scale having these nailed will become even more essential. Pennies on your calculations translate to valuable % margins on your bottom line which are critical especially when you are pitching to larger retailers.

Pricing

Each step along the way, as I am sure you will have gleaned to this point, is hugely important. That said, getting the price right (or wrong) can keep or (cut off) the oxygen to your business. Once you have your costs, you then need to create your pricing structure.

Are you selling direct?

This would be at a show, market or festival. For instance, I was able to sell 3 x 100g bags for £6 when at the likes of BBC Good Food, whereas in general retail the RRP and sale price was £2.49.

Are you selling to distributors?

When this is the case you have two margins to factor in. One for the distributor, and the other for their customer (the retailer).

Are you selling to multiples where you will need to factor in promotions?

Retailers in the main will expect that you partake in some of the promotions in their yearly calendar. Typically, it will work out to be 12 weeks of the year on a margin maintained basis, i.e. you as the producer take the hit on your margin, not them.

What are your competitors selling at?

I am not suggesting that you have to be identical to your competitors, indeed Scrubbys' main competition in mainstream impulse category for snacking was Tyrrells. They retailed at £1.99 for 150g. Scrubbys were £2.49 for 100g. So, as you can see, we were at a premium; 0.024 v 0.013 per 100g.

What I am saying, though, is that you will need to be in the same ballpark.

What size or weight is your product? The RRP you will have in mind is just that, 'in mind', and 'recommended' – you cannot dictate the retail price when you're selling to the retailers; this is illegal!

I stress this point as due to my lack of knowledge and experience I made this very mistake with Planet Organic. I secured the listing (as usual a hard-won one). Part of the listing agreement was to launch with a programme of edible marketing (in-store sampling).

I turned up to the first store and saw Scrubbys on sale for £1.99. I was furious. I didn't want them out there in retail at that price because I knew to make my margins stack up later when I was in major retail they needed to be out there at £2.49 as I would be factoring in promotions.

I contacted my buyer with the demand that they retail at £2.49. I was swiftly told that what I'd just done was illegal, and did I know. I explained that no, I didn't, and promptly apologised and backed down.

What you can do, however, which is what I should have done to try and govern what they would retail at, is to sell at a price where they are pushed to retail at your RRP or higher. Either that or they take a hit on their margin. Our distributors went out with a higher RRP. Harrods (I know this is an extreme example) retailed at £2.99.

Sales channels/routes to market

You will most likely have multiple channels/routes to market, and you need to know what the margin expectations are for each, and to a degree your costs could help identify which channels to choose, i.e. it's pointless targeting discounters and pound shops if your costs come in above a pound! Routes to market are typically:

<u>Retailers</u>
Ocado, Waitrose, Sainsbury's, Tesco, Morrisons, Asda etc.

<u>Distributors</u>
Cotswold Fayre, The Cress Co, Hider Foods, Suma, Marigold Health Foods, Diverse Fine Foods etc.

<u>Garden Centre Groups</u> (you can go direct to these, but some/most buy through distributors)

Dobbies, Wyevale Garden Centres, Notcutts, British Garden Centres (there are more).

<u>Travel: rail and air</u>
East Coast Trains, British Airways, Hull Trains, DHL, easyJet (again there are more, but just to give you a picture).

<u>Fashion retailers</u>
Primark, New Look, River Island, Next etc.

Buyers

Depending on your product, and if you are aiming at securing listings with the major retailers, there may be a number of buyers you can approach. For instance, with Scrubbys I could approach:

- Free From
- Impulse (main crisps aisle)
- Food to Go (for 40g single serve bags)

A kick-ass presentation is a must, within which you should include:

- An intro
  - About you
  - About your product
  - About your brand
- Category statistics
  - From a consumer point of view
  - From a product point of view
- Size of the market data
- Size of the opportunity you have identified

- How your product fits
  - Within the market
  - Within the category
- What you are bringing to the category
- Who your consumer is
- How you are going to communicate to your consumer/drive them to the retailer
- A marketing plan
- Commercials including promotions etc.

Don't just have meaningless slides, though. No one wants death by PowerPoint; make each slide count. When I am working with my clients I have a number of varying presentations, and tailor them for buyer and sales channel, and this is what I would suggest you do too.

Profit and margins

You need to make a profit, the distributor (if you choose that route) needs to make a profit, and the retailer needs to make a profit... it's all about the profit!

Each step along the way, costs need to be covered and a margin added for the profit. There are industry standards of what the profit margin looks like for each route. These can vary per category too.

Cashflow

I am sure you don't need this reiterating here, but at the risk of telling your grandmother how to suck eggs – cashflow is the priority; you can't get from where you are to where you want to go without it!

STEP 7:
Marketing Your Product

Raise awareness

You've got all the ingredients in place: your product, your brand, your costs, your prices. Now it's time to lift the roof and get your product out there! How do you plan to do this? I am sure you can incorporate some of the activity which I've shared worked for me.

Have you devised a marketing strategy? If not, you need to. Knowing your product and category inside out is vital. Have a full understanding of your product and brand so you can communicate this effectively.

Marketing

Your marketing activity is required for both the end consumer and your customers (retailers and distributors). What's your story? This could be you as the founder i.e. why you created your brand and product, or about your actual product, the ingredients etc. – are they unusual? Is your cooking/production method different?

A lot of my clients don't drill down enough to understanding who their customer is – who is the end consumer? It's really tempting to say 'Everyone – everyone eats, right?!' Wrong! Yes, of course we all eat, but you need to spend time and narrow down exactly who your consumer is; exactly who is buying and eating your product?

Once you know who your target is, then you should spend time thinking about how you can reach them, and what will motivate them to buy.

The basic 4 Ps of Marketing are:

- Product
- Price
- Promotion
- Place

Product – Food is fast moving, with the market changing constantly along with the needs and desires of consumers. Keep up to date with what is happening in your category and the wider market to remain current and relevant. Your business success hangs a lot on getting your product offering right.

Price – Your product needs to be priced accordingly, and should be representative to your category, competitors and your brand, i.e. not a world away from other products in the category, and what people would expect to pay in the category, and in keeping with your brand.

Promotion – Define the message about your brand from the off and be consistent with the promotion of this message to effectively communicate to your consumers.

Place – Where do your consumers hang out? Where is the right place to shout your message? Have a good think about your brand, its voice, its style... what kind of marketing will complement this?

There are many platforms you could think of to use: social media, bloggers and key influencers. Which forms of media will your consumers see? How can you get your brand and product in front of them and convince them to buy your product?

Edible marketing

This could be on a market stall, at a food festival, in-store sampling at your local farm shop/deli. Once you have engaged your customers in sampling, you stand a much better chance of converting them to buy, and repeat buy too. As a standard rule of thumb, when I sampled Scrubbys in store an uplift of sales continued for around six weeks thereafter.

On pack

Remember you can communicate a great deal of information on your product packaging so don't overlook what can be included on here. Take care not to overcrowd though; pick three key messages to shout.

Your packaging material can contribute to the overall brand message too, so give thought to how you could use this to your advantage and in cooperation to convey your message.

Press release

Now is a good time to have a press release written: preparation ready to meet the opportunity! Start reading publications you would like to be featured in, look for the journalist name, also dig journalists out on social media. It's a good idea to have some good pack shot images at this stage too.

Real Account

HOW I'VE HELPED AND
WORKED WITH A FOOD BUSINESS

My name is Susan Gafsen and I started Pep & Lekker about 18 months ago, with my sister-in-law, having finished an MBA, and looking for a new challenge and direction in my life.

I had worked for 25 years in the City in leading law firms, first as a corporate lawyer and then in business development and marketing. From those very first days as a corporate lawyer advising entrepreneurs I wanted to have my own business, and if I'm honest was a bit envious.

I had never previously had the courage to start my own business, but with the confidence of an MBA distinction behind me, and being in my early 50s, thought if not now then when?

Pep & Lekker came into being as my son became vegan and I was frustrated by the tasteless and processed food available and didn't like buying him food that no one else in the family wanted to eat.

My husband and I were also moving over to a plant-based dairy-free diet and so I wanted to make food that could be enjoyed by all of us, and was really healthy. My family are all lovers of soup and this seemed a good place to start.

I came to work with Claire as the challenges of starting a new brand, out of my own pocket, in a sector that I knew nothing about, became overwhelming.

I had reached out to a mentor before and that had not worked out, but I realised that in this highly competitive market I needed to grow and could not stand still and I would need to crowdfund.

I knew that I had to get my house in order before I could even consider this a possibility. I found Claire by searching on a website called Foodhub and from our first conversation realised that she was just what I needed and we would be a great fit.

The main problems that I had were really getting an understanding of:

- What my margins should realistically be at this stage of my business and how to drive costs down
- My costs of production are high with my low volumes and the delivery charges are crippling with a chilled product on timing and level of promotions
- Setting RRPs
- Driving sales and identifying appropriate targets
- Social media and PR

Juliette and I had an amazing meeting with Claire where she provided practical solutions to our immediate problems to action and suggestions for a way forward. Within 24 hours Claire followed up with a summary of our meeting, an action plan, an email to retailers and a slide of sales targets.

Soup was a great place to start, but we always had ideas on adding to the brand offering of Pep & Lekker to include savoury organic seed snacks, which we have now launched. Claire has been of invaluable help, support and assistance with this too.

She has also been available by email to respond to any crisis that I may have and provides me with workable solutions. I feel so much calmer and more able to cope, and I am confident that with Claire I will be able to drive things forward.

With Claire, I have found a person that for a long time will be my mentor, and hopefully in due course, my confidant and friend.

Susan Gafsen | Co-Founder Pep & Lekker
www.pepandlekker.com

What Would Claire Do Now?

In terms of pitching to buyers I'd have had a more bespoke approach to each of them. The sell to a farm shop/deli is very different from the sell into the retailers.

Farm shops and deli buyers are in the main a more friendly and approachable bunch. I am not saying the retailers aren't, but they're driven by different dynamics. The emphasis with the retailers is very much more category driven.

As a producer/brand founder it's all too easy to be 'blinded' by your passion. It's a given that your product tastes amazing. Whose product tastes like shit, no one's, right?! So, what are you going to do to stand out from the other brands who are pitching and competing for the shelf space too?

I'd have researched other routes to market more thoroughly, and not just, as a lot of new food brands do, thought only of the major retailers. There are some very healthy and well-known brands out there who have built their business without even going to the retailers.

Although I had some knowledge on this, it was cashflow pressures which made me want to snare a big listing. I think the problems arise from really planning in the outset how you'll grow, the time this will take, and being realistic on cash – you are back to what I shared earlier; please do not try and brush over the things which you should do.

Looking back, we had lots stacked against us from the off, not least of all on our margins. So, I would always say make sure you have a healthy margin and aren't setting yourself up for added challenges from a cashflow perspective by these being too small.

If you'd told me this back then, I wouldn't have listened, because I was adamant on what I wanted to achieve. But I maintain to this day that certain decisions I made and actions I took made for a much bumpier and at times traumatic road than it could and should have been.

Claire's Diamond

Innovation plus positive disruption = the best chance of success.

Exercise:

What YOU should do now

What are your COGS? – Write them down here.
Pricing – Make a list of the different prices you think you'll have.
Sales channels – What are your routes to market, and who are your sales targets; which buyers are you targeting?

Work out what your margins and profits look like for each of the routes to market.

Raise awareness – What is your plan?

Marketing – Make a skeleton list of all the platforms you intend to use, then translate this to a full 360 degree marketing plan.

CHAPTER 6

A Dream, a Business... but Broke

*L*ooking for a job led me to meet another industry leader whom I now have the pleasure of being connected to: Jane Milton. Jane is a powerhouse in the world of food, and I am extremely grateful to her for the number of times she has helped and advised me now.

You can see a theme here of me having the good fortune along my journey of meeting and remaining very good friends with several influential people. This is something I never take for granted. Each one of these people has worked and fought hard to be where they are in the industry and their business. You must **take care of and respect your network as you are building it.** I am sure we have all heard the saying, your network is your net worth.

I reached out to Jane on my job securing mission. This reaped a reward in the guise of being put forward for a job, which I was later offered with one of her clients. This client, ProperMaid, just happened to have Deborah Meaden on the board of her business as one of the investors.

Deborah is one of the five 'Dragons' on the BBC TV show *Dragons' Den*, and Deborah invested in ProperMaid after they pitched on the show. I remember watching the pitch, not thinking at the time that it would be something I would consider doing.

At the same time as applying for other jobs, and after a couple of interviews, I was offered the position of national sales manager for a company in Bradford, Gordon Rhodes.

I now found myself having two job offers, but also an opportunity to pitch on *Dragons' Den*.

When the phone rang that day, following my distraction from my book-keeping, it was the researcher, Fran, returning my call. I was on the phone with her for what seemed like an age. She asked questions along the lines of:

- What are your manufacturing costs per unit?
- What is the wholesale price per unit?
- What is the retail price per unit?
- What is your turnover to date?
- What is your gross profit to date?
- What is your net profit to date?
- What are your forecasts of gross, net and turnover for the next three years?
- How much would you like to pitch for?
- What would you do with the investment if you secured it?

- What is your exit strategy?
- Who is your target market?

The questions were in-depth, and a lot of detailed knowledge was required 'on the spot'. I clearly answered them all to the required standard as she asked if she could speak to my husband (as the other partner in the business) who was out at the time.

When John came in, he saw that 'look' on my face and asked me what I'd done. Although he wasn't sold on the idea at that point, he agreed to ring Fran back.

Their conversation went along the same lines as the conversation I'd had. At the end of the call it was left that should they want to invite us to Manchester for auditions they'd be in touch soon.

It was soon. We received an email after a few days inviting us to Media City in Manchester to audition. We had no idea what to expect; neither of us had any TV experience at all. We'd done radio and I'd got lots of speaking gigs under my belt by this time, but it's a whole new ball game when you're looking at a camera.

I remember we had to have an 'elevator pitch' ready for the day, to say to the camera. It was along the lines, but a shorter version, of what you'd say should you get through to being selected for the show.

We had that all prepped and ready, but I don't mind admitting that it took us quite a few takes to get it right, to the point where I didn't think we'd done a good enough job and wasn't confident that we'd made it through this stage. By the end of this session though I had got quite good... TV, no worries!

It turned out to be good enough. I received a phone call from Fran after only a few days; we had made it through and were invited to pitch.

At the audition we were asked to sign a whole dossier of paperwork. It all really amounted to the same thing: that we wouldn't tell anyone should we be successful in being chosen to go through to the show, and if we leaked it in any way we were in danger of being sued.

One of the stipulations was you couldn't know or have any contact with any of the Dragons. All of this was happening simultaneously – the job offer via Jane Milton with ProperMaid, with Deborah Meaden on the board, the job offer at Gordon Rhodes, and the nod to say we'd got through to pitch on *Dragons' Den*. I was in a whirl; literally within days of each other, all of this was going on.

I had to think fast. My decision around the jobs and *Dragons' Den* had the stipulation of not being connected to a Dragon at the heart of it. I was torn; I knew John wasn't as keen on the *Dragons' Den* prospect as I was.

Decisions, decisions; if I took the job with Deborah Meaden on the board, would I get to meet her, and potentially approach her as an investor independent of *Dragons' Den*? Was this even an option, or would she be interested? If I took the job, and accepted *Dragons' Den*, and it was found out that I had a link, albeit tenuous, to a Dragon, would I not be able to pursue *Dragons' Den* further?

Do I take the other job with Gordon Rhodes job, and accept the pitch to *Dragons' Den*? I would feel bad keeping *Dragons' Den* from my employer, but this seemed the best decision; I would have a chance to meet all five Dragons, and the Gordon Rhodes job came with a car. This was a godsend as our car was on its last legs and we couldn't afford another.

I turned down the ProperMaid job, and told Jane it was due to the other job offer, and it was the car which had swayed it. You may remember I had signed to say that I wouldn't tell anyone that I'd been selected to pitch on *Dragons' Den*.

This time frame was one of the most stressful times for me. My stress levels soared. I was being crushed by holding down a full-time national sales manager job with a 150-mile round trip commute plus running and growing Scrubbys, and having the kids at key points in their lives where they needed so much time and input from me – GCSEs for Lucy, option choices for Abigail and primary school SATS for George.

My plan of being able to cross-sell to some contacts worked well. On some occasions in meetings with buyers, certainly the distributor accounts, I was able to talk about Scrubbys and Gordon Rhodes, thereby in effect using my time twice. Gordon Rhodes knew this and were very supportive as I was able to use my Scrubbys contacts to pull sales over to them too, so it was working very well.

I felt awful not being able to tell them that I'd applied for and would soon be pitching on *Dragons' Den*, but there are times when you have to do what is best for you. This was one of those occasions.

The day of filming came around. I should have known for a couple of reasons that all wasn't going to end well. I was under pressure from a client for a meeting on the same date as the filming. I was able to put it back, but only for a day. It was one of my biggest accounts so I had to keep them on side. So, no matter what happened in the Den, I had a 400-mile round trip ahead of me the next day.

Also, the pitching date was the 1st April – April Fool's Day, not a good omen!

We'd had some bespoke crisp packets made for each of the Dragons. We had their pictures on the crisp bags, along with a 'catchy' sentence about them and their business interests as follows:

- Peter Jones Scrubbys – Larger than average vegetable crisps for Peter's conference
- Deborah Meaden's Scrubbys – Deliciously dippable vegetable crisps for Deborah's shindig
- Duncan Bannatyne's Scrubbys – Healthy and nutritious vegetable crisps for Duncan's club
- Piers Linney's Scrubbys – Fresh and natural vegetable crisps for Piers' party
- Kelly Hoppen's Scrubbys – Sophisticated vegetable crisps with class for Kelly's studio

We had decided to set the studio up with vegetables, hessian, trestle table, crisps, pop-up banners etc, similar to how we would present ourselves at shows. We'd done a practice set-up in our conservatory at home to play around with what we thought would look best.

If you live more than a certain number of miles away from where *Dragons' Den* is filmed (Manchester) the show producers ask you to stay the night before filming; we fell into this category. So we packed the car the afternoon before the day of filming: all our stuff, props, crisps etc. etc.

Neither of us slept very well that night in the hotel. We'd been given instructions to be dressed in our pitching clothes (business dress), hair and makeup done (in my case!) and be in the hotel reception at 6am the next morning. It was there we met some of the other entrepreneurs for that day.

We arrived at the Den. The night before after checking into the hotel we'd taken all our stand and pitch stuff, so that was there ready. We'd also supplied a photograph for the show/studio staff of the practice set-up we'd done so they knew in the studio how we wanted the stand set.

It was around 7.30am when we were shown into the 'green room'. This is where we would be along with all other entrepreneurs pitching on the day until we were required on set. Not long afterwards we, along with all the other entrepreneurs, were asked to go to the set where each of our lift scenes could be filmed.

After that a long wait unfolded for us. None of us knew the running order of the pitches; it was a case of waiting until you were called. As I am sure you can imagine, all you can do is run through your pitch continually, chat amongst yourselves and get increasingly nervous.

Lunchtime came and went. Early afternoon came and went. It got to the point where it was touch and go as to whether we would get on to pitch or not, or if it would get too late.

By this time, it had got to around 5pm. I rang my mum to explain what was happening – she was at home looking after the kids – as I knew she'd be wondering why I'd not been in touch.

John and I were the very last people in the green room. We'd watched all the entrepreneurs go one by one. Once you've pitched you don't go back into the green room; you leave the building. With this being the case, we'd no idea who, if any, had secured investment that day, or what it was like. You are kept in the dark the entire time.

We then got word that we were up. A quick sit in the hair and makeup chair, then we were off. My heart was pounding. I had absolutely everything pinned on this pitch. I was bone exhausted in the lead-up to this; this was the most critical point in our business to date.

Even though I had my sales job at Gordon Rhodes, I hadn't let up in my focus on sales with Scrubbys. Through this I had managed to get a commitment to list from both Ocado and Waitrose. This was amazing, and what I had been striving for, for so long. It brought with it pressures, though.

I'd secured what should have been the listing which changed our fortunes: Waitrose, two lines in 200 stores nationwide. What's the problem, I hear you say? Well we didn't have enough packaging, or enough cash, to originate the plates and packaging for a new variant, which I'd committed to when asked by the buyer.

Waitrose wanted to list the original four vegetable mix and the parsnip with chilli & lime in 40g bags (which wasn't available in this size at the time of pitching, but I agreed to it anyway to get the listing). This was just one of the reasons why we so desperately needed the investment and a Dragon on board.

I wasn't just there for the brand publicity as some entrepreneurs so clearly are; I was there for survival. I was exhausted and thought if we could get a Dragon on board with all their expertise and connections we could pull away. I could leave my job and 100% devote my time to Scrubbys. I won't say focus; I was focused, and to be honest this was to the detriment of our family, marriage and the kids. Cracks were showing all round.

We walked into the Den, and I recited my pitch which I'd practised hundreds of times:

> *Hello, Dragons. I'm Claire, and this is my husband John. We are here today to ask for £75,000 in return for 15% equity in our business, Scrubbys Vegetable Crisps. Our crisps are at least 30% less fat and 18% less calories than standard fried vegetable crisps.*
>
> *They are also gluten-free. We launched Scrubbys in May 2012 with the intention of bringing a healthier snacking option to the market, and we are on a mission to bring healthier snacking to the masses.*
>
> *The UK snacking market is ever growing and is currently worth £3.3 billion, with the crisp sector worth £930 million. We've got some great*

high-profile listings to date, namely Harrods, Fortnum & Mason and Partridges.

Our crisps have been awarded a gold star at the Great Taste Awards and Scrubbys has been named a CoolBrand. We have secured a listing with the online supermarket Ocado. And we are also launching into circa 200 Waitrose stores in the 'free-from' section.

I then went on to hand the personalised crisp packets to each Dragon. They all, without exception, liked the crisps and complimented us on the branding and product. The questions came thick and fast. We were asked all the usual ones which have seen other entrepreneurs unravel: the finance ones all around margins, profits and turnover.

We had all our facts and figures bang on, no unravelling for us. Duncan (Bannatyne) came in with an offer: half of the money for half of the equity. The rules of the Den are that if you don't secure the full amount you have pitched for then no deal is done. So, pressure and tension was sky-high as we were fighting to try and get another Dragon to commit.

Deborah (Meaden), despite being complimentary about us as people, and the product, declared herself out: *'I see the pressure on this business from every single side. So, as a business decision, I won't be making you an offer. So, I'm out.'* Deborah could see the strain we were under as the spotlight had been turned on us personally and our financial situation. She wasn't wrong; she could clearly see the pressure and emotion I was trying desperately but unsuccessfully to hide.

Next up was Piers (Linney): *'I still think that the ship has sailed slightly on this one. I just don't think it's going to scale the way you think it might. I'm out.'* Piers was wrong; he was like the others we had encountered along the way, mainly in the very early days. Not only had the ship not sailed; it hadn't left shore. Just look at how the healthier snacking category had exploded since 2014. This shows that no one gets it right 100% of the time... not even the all-knowing Dragons in the Den.

It was then time for Kelly (Hoppen) to declare where she was: *'Part of me is sitting here with my heart and then there's the business side of me. But I can't sit in this chair and make a commitment to you that I can make this work if I don't honestly think that I can. So, it's with sadness, but I'm afraid I'm out.'*

We were then left with Peter to declare his position. Whilst I was stood looking at Peter, my mind would wander back to the MADE Festival where I had stood very eager, very naive and very innocent to what the coming few years would take out of me. Of course, there's no way he would remember me, but I remembered that encounter.

Peter asked us how we were surviving. Had we got other jobs or were we just doing this...? I told him candidly where we were at, and that a few weeks ago, we hit the wall, and I'd taken a job. He then spoke the words that haunted me and played in my head for a long time after:

'It's written all over Claire's face. It's taken you to the edge, hasn't it? You've gone back to work, to support your family. You've got a dream. You've got a business... but you're broke.'

This really shook me, and if you saw the airing on TV, you'll know I was close to tears. By this time, we'd been in the Den for over an hour. In total we were in there just under two hours, much longer than the edited 11 minutes which were aired on TV.

A conversation then broke out between Peter, Duncan and myself. It was clear that Duncan wanted Peter on board; he wanted to do the deal with Peter coming in with the remaining £37,500.

Then Peter delivered the body blow to declare himself out: *'John, Claire, I'm sorry, I can't do it. It would be really wrong of me. It's going against everything that is right in my own business head, to do the deal, so I'm going to tell you unfortunately I'm out.'*

That was it then. I recall thinking 'We're screwed, where do we go from here?' My mind was a riot. I had pinned all the hope I could muster on securing investment in the Den, and for it not to happen was devastating.

We left Manchester, a 2½ hour drive home, and I cried the whole journey.

I was done; that was it. I couldn't see a way through it. I was physically and mentally exhausted. We arrived back home; the kids were in bed. Good job, I didn't want them to see me so upset. I went to bed, not for long though;

I had my appointment with that 400-mile round trip to uphold with my Gordon Rhodes customer.

I pretty much couldn't hold it together for the next two weeks. I simply felt like I was 'shit at life'. No one or nothing could convince me otherwise.

I was shot, finished, done. I lost all hope. This journey had been so hard, relentless, and it showed no sign of taking a turn for the better, and that was a thought I simply couldn't cope with. This business with the stresses and strains was ravaging me, John, our kids, our marriage and our family.

What did I do then? How DID I cope? Well, I did what anyone would do: **'If you're going through hell, keep going'** as Winston Churchill had so wisely said.

Easy words eh. It was time for me to take a dose of my own medicine and have a word with myself. Self-talk myself with some of the insights and tips I've shared with you throughout this book. I'm not saying it was easy; it wasn't. I went back in my head to surviving my blood clot. If I could get through that I am damn sure I can get through this. That WAS life and death; this isn't.

Yes, it could have potentially been the end of Scrubbys. All that hard work, determination and rising to each and every challenge would have been wasted in the sense that we wouldn't have succeeded, but not in the sense of what we had already learned on the way – you see nothing is ever wasted. It's only when you look back that you can join the dots.

But I wasn't done, not by a long shot. I picked myself up and came back stronger. With the emotion dying down after time I was able to get my rational head back on, make some decisions with a clear head, no emotion, and think on what to do.

We had lots of positives to work with:

- Sales were increasing.
- We were a credible, reputable multi award-winning brand.
- We had just secured Ocado and Waitrose.

There must be a way to secure investment from other avenues. So, I started once more to look for investors. The clock was ticking though. This was April, and the Waitrose launch was to be August, so time to do some big thinking…

The Practical Stuff

Now you've gone through steps 1–7, you may well be at the stage where you're wanting to grow, and invariably this is the stage when investment is sought to do just that. Using my experience of pitching for investment at all stages, and in varying different situations, here's my advice.

I know from my own experience, which I have shared with you, that raising finance in your business is one of the hardest challenges a lot of entrepreneurs face. The food world is one in which the percentage of businesses requiring funding is high.

There are several business models where you don't need much, if any cash to launch with, but food often isn't one of these, from my own personal experience, and working with my clients.

What I will say though, and always advise my clients, the moment you have someone else in your business you are beholden to them. Their goals come into the business as well as your own.

Here is my advice for successfully pitching for investment.

1. **Know exactly what you need the money for.**
   What you are going to spend it on? You should have a full breakdown. What will the return for the investor be? No investor will give you the time of day if you don't have answers to these questions. To be honest, nor should they. If you

don't have the answers you don't have a solid plan or model. Would you invest any of your hard-earned cash to someone who couldn't answer these questions? No, I didn't think so.

2. **Build your network way in advance of being at the stage where you need investment.**

Work on the scenario that at some point you will need to pitch. That way you're prepared. If you don't, well then that's a bonus. By doing this, you won't be at the stage where your back is against the wall having to take the wrong deal through time pressures if you are prepared in advance. From the experience I now have, a lot of your chances of securing investment do come through your connections.

3. **How have your competitors raised their investment?**

Is this something you can model too? I remember when I was looking for investment, crowdfunding was just taking off. My gut was that this would be a good option for us. I ran this idea past someone who should have been in the know and placed to advise me. He advised against it, and I stupidly went against my gut and followed what I now see as the wrong advice. I would also recommend that you keep up to date with what the government is offering for entrepreneurs. I recall when SEIS (the Seed Enterprise Investment Scheme) was introduced; I quickly made sure that Scrubbys was eligible for this, making us attractive to investors.

4. **There are many funding options coming up all the time.**

Keep your ear to the ground, and again investigate your network. Look to other food businesses raising investment, and ask what they are doing. These can include invoice financing. Here are some, and other facilities too. Some I have worked with, and others I have directed clients to:

- www.gapcap.co.uk
- www.kickstarter.com
- www.startuploans.co.uk
- www.virginstartup.org
- www.primestox.com
- www.jamjarinvestments.co.uk
- www.piper.co.uk
- www.crowdcube.com
- www.seedrs.com
- www.crowdfooding.co.uk

5. **Be confident and let your passion shine.**

No one is going to invest in you or your business if you aren't giving the right vibes. They need to have faith in you, your brand, your product and your business. Don't spend time in your pitch highlighting risks associated with your business. Lead with upsides, and give who you're pitching to a reason to be excited.

6. **On the flip side, don't over-egg.**

By this I mean, don't have pie in the sky figures and unrealistic goals; your potential investors will see straight through this. It's worth remembering that invariably they've been there and done it. They're not able to be hoodwinked. Transparency is key.

7. **Understand your business inside out.**
You need to have a firm handle on all the key metrics. These include:

- Who your customer is
- How you reach your customer
- Know all your margins
- Know your cashflow
- Be able to communicate your supply chain effectively from production to delivery

8. **Know what you want from an investor.**
I am asked this a lot by my clients – where can I find investment? Well a lot depends on what you are looking for. Are you simply wanting cash, or do you want someone in your business who brings cash and expertise? Do you want the cash to come with someone having an input into your business, or simply a shareholder who will just sit at a distance on the board to be furnished with figures and reports as they demand? Likewise, is it cash you need, or do you need someone like me to mentor you, to find solutions and ways to work through the pinch you are possibly in?

9. **Don't switch your potential off before you've even switched them on.**
What do I mean by this? Don't blag. If you don't know the answer to a question I would always recommend being honest. Tell them you don't know, you will find the answer and get back to

them. Don't be arrogant; if your ego is too big they will instantly switch off. There is a huge difference between having passion in your business and being arrogant. Be honest about yourself and your business too. If you have made mistakes to date in your business (which let's face it, all of us have at some point) don't try and cover them up. Admit to them, own up, but always share what you have learnt from them. This can make you more investable: the investor isn't funding your mistakes, since you've already paid for them with your own cash.

10. **It's a two-way street.**
Don't jump into bed with the first (investor) that comes along. In my experience anyone you work with in your business on this level is someone you must feel 100% comfortable with. You will be spending more time with them than your closest family members or partner. I cannot express strongly enough that a good relationship from both sides of the table is paramount.

Real Account

HOW I'VE HELPED AND
WORKED WITH A FOOD BUSINESS

It all started when we made changes to our own diets, which had positive impacts on us. We then struggled to find 'good' food options when we were out at various events and realised that having something 'good' meant having to make it yourself.

We started Pure Recharge in 2013 to provide better food options. Initially we made healthy home cook meals and smoothies at sports events. We soon realised that our smoothies were our USP and thing we loved making the most. We made our own recipes for superfood smoothies, which could be prepared quickly and reduced waste associated with smoothies. We soon realised we wanted to reach people beyond events, so that our customers could make our smoothies conveniently at home. Our smoothie pouches allowed them to still enjoy the great tastes, increase in energy and wellbeing which our smoothies promoted.

From about a year into our business, up until we met Claire, we had consultations with various other business mentors, but they didn't seem to 'get us' or the vision of what the products and company were about. We thought mentors may have not been the direction for us, until we came across Claire's details on a food business Facebook group.

When we read Claire's story, something about it resonated with us, so we reached out to contact her. After a 30-minute call, it was apparent she knew exactly where we were as a business, what we were up against and what we wanted to achieve. The following day we sent her a sample of our products and have not looked back since.

Before we met Claire we had been working on Pure Recharge as a hobby that had future potential. It had reached the stage where we were overwhelmed with the amount of things we needed to do and it was becoming too much to run alongside our day jobs. We had been working hard but struggled to get traction. By the end of 2017 we had hit a wall; we were exhausted, and the business either needed to turn a corner and become self-sustaining or become just one of life's anecdotes.

After Claire tried our smoothies, we had an initial video chat. Claire quickly understood what we were about, but recognised we lacked direction. She took what we had done so far and got us to build on it, rather than trying to restructure it. Through an iterative process of implementing manageable tasks and goals, we are now starting to find our path and what works best for us.

Claire actually listens to our feedback on how things have gone, also by having someone to report back to she keeps us on track.

Fundamentally and most importantly she helped us believe in our company! And helped us realise that we could make it happen! Even when things haven't worked out as we hoped, she helps us review, consolidate, dust off and get back out there for another round!

She has helped us develop different techniques to help us engage with our audience. We now seek help where we need it, instead of trying to do it all ourselves. Claire has helped save us from decision fatigue and mulling things over endlessly. Now we are more direct in our activities and have a structured approach to how we will achieve our outcomes. We now regularly review the impact of each approach after trying it.

Even if there are two co-founders of a business, you need the outside influence of someone who sees things objectively, but at the same time does not extinguish the emotion and passion which created it in the first place.

Although our journey with Claire has only just begun, we have gained a lot of ground, which we may not have had the patience to reach on our own.

Dara and Joe | Founders of Pure Recharge
www.purerecharge.com

What Would Claire Do Now?

Would I still have done *Dragons' Den* is THE one question I am repeatedly asked. The answer is yes.

Why? – because it gave amazing leverage to the brand. I believe to this day that it gave the best launch platform any brand could have.

One with the zero-marketing budget that is. We were extremely lucky that the airing of *Dragons' Den* coincided with the Waitrose launch and a Carfest festival we were exhibiting at.

I remember people coming up to me at the stand at Carfest and asking me if I was OK. The reason was that the clip that the BBC used for the advert was me fighting back tears after my Peter Jones grilling.

I would enter the process in a different way though. Through not being in the show foremost for the publicity – I was hell-bent on securing investment – I had neglected to take on board mentally the 'reality' TV aspect of it. I would have 'played the game' and gone in with this brain. I was too raw, too emotional and too attached to the outcome.

I would always advise that in anything you undertake don't be wedded to an outcome. Chill out, relax more. In my experience now the more I adopt that attitude the better outcomes I get. It may feel counterintuitive, but it works.

Claire's Diamond

See what happens when you push through and dig deep; hold your mettle and keep the faith.

If anyone is contemplating *Dragons' Den*, this would be my advice:

- Know every single aspect of your business inside out, back to front and in between.
- Be prepared to be stood in front of the Dragons for hours.
- Be prepared for about 60 people and multiple cameras filming you at the same time.
- Bear in mind that whilst one Dragon is asking you a question which you're replying to, the other four are thinking of their questions; therefore, the questions come thick and fast. There is no let-up. This is partly why when edited down you see the entrepreneurs looking at times very flustered. The Dragons have a lot of thinking time in comparison to the entrepreneur.
- Really understand that you have no control whatsoever about how you are going to be edited. It's a TV show after all, and they want good TV, which means at times they want controversy, drama, tension and suspense.
- Try and relax. I know this sounds a bit daft. I think though that had I not been so stressed I may have had a different outcome. They are very astute and perceptive people; you can't hoodwink them. I tried to hide my emotion, the stress and strain, but I was fooling no one.

I'd have handled Waitrose better. You mustn't be afraid to push back and negotiate. By lack of negotiation and not working to the natural flow of where my business was, I committed to the parsnip with chilli & lime in the 40g bag which put added strain on the business.

I did this because we needed the listing, and from that we needed volume. It's all well and good me saying this now though. Had I pushed back, perhaps I wouldn't have got the listing, and at that time to be honest I think it would have been sudden death for the brand. So, I took the risk, took the chance, and we will never know how it would've worked out had I not done this.

I think when dealing with retailers, and any buyer in general, do not underestimate your ability to negotiate. Be strong on that. Stand your ground. Understand your commercials. You are better to walk away if the timing is off (if your business can stand that) rather than be a busy fool.

The other way to look at it is to take the punt, with the brain that if you get a good listing under your belt, that could possibly be the stepping stone you are looking for to get you to your next listing. It's only a possibly; there are never any guarantees. You must as always understand yourself, your product, your brand, your commercials, your business and your cashflow.

There is no rule of thumb. This is why it's a good thing to have someone on board as a mentor. When you try and make these decisions alone it can be hard to work through. Not least when you are a passionate producer, who in fact can be blinded by that very passion.

Exercise:

What YOU should do now

If you're at the stage where you're planning to raise investment, have you thought where to look? Write your options and thoughts down here:
What do you think you need the investment for? Make a list of exactly what you will use the investment for.
How much money do you think you need to raise? What amount is allocated to each of the things you need?

Are you looking for loan investment or to build a team of support? Make a list of what support you think you need if that is the case.

Have you thought about what equity you are happy to sell? Write down your current share structure here, and what you think that might look like with investors on board.

CHAPTER 7

Turning the
Longest Corner,
Sweet but Bitter

*A*s I've shared, along our journey we'd picked up several connections and contacts.

Another occasion was one day whilst I was sampling in a deli stockist in Harrogate. A gentleman came to taste the crisps and started to ask some questions about them, but what he was asking wasn't the usual kind of questions I normally faced when sampling.

You probably know by now that I am not one to hold back or not speak my mind, so I asked him what he really wanted to know; what did his questions mean? He asked me if we were looking for investment for the business and gave me his details.

I decided to contact him, and answered his question, that yes, we were looking for investment. This led to him putting us in touch with a group of investors. We contacted them, and it was agreed that they come over to meet with us at the E-Factor offices in Grimsby, and then subsequent meetings followed. These had all taken place before *Dragons' Den*, and we decided to walk away as we weren't happy with the terms they were requesting.

Once you've filmed *Dragons' Den*, you have no idea of the timescale between pitch and TV airing, or indeed if you are even going to get any airtime at all, or how much you will get if you do. I remember watching the episode when it was aired, and a couple of the entrepreneurs we'd been in the green room with literally got a few seconds on TV where Evan Davis (the show presenter) simply said something like 'Others who tried and failed in the den...'.

In our case we filmed on the 1st April and aired 20th July. That's not too long a time frame, however when you're running out of time from a cashflow perspective with your back against the wall it is.

I was trying to keep sales coming in and hold down a demanding job. Every day felt like a month. Even more so when I didn't know what timescales I was facing.

So, with no idea if we were going to get any airtime (in which case we may or may not have had exposure to other potential investors) or when this may be, or whether we were lucky enough to make the final cut, we had to think about how we could get some investment to fulfil the Ocado and Waitrose listings.

Our minds went back to the investors we had walked away from pre-*Dragons' Den*. We'd taken the kids out for the day, some much needed family time out of the business. Yes, out of the business physically, but not

Claire's Diamond

Never go back; there is nothing good there. If something was meant to be it would've been.

mentally. John and I were talking, and we decided that yes, albeit a bit reluctantly, we'd contact these investors again.

A meeting was agreed a few days later in York. The meeting went well. We shared the listing commitments from Ocado and Waitrose, and how the business was generally growing and progressing.

A few more meetings resulted in a deal being put on the table. As before it wasn't one we were happy with, because we were going to have to sell a larger proportion of the business than we wanted to. At that point we really couldn't see any other way forward.

There was a choice in one sense: go with it, or lose everything, however this didn't feel like a choice at all. To say it was an extremely hard thing to do is a huge understatement, and it took some getting our heads around; this was our baby, but ultimately at the time it felt like it was the right thing for the brand.

We just managed to cling on to majority, but when all was done, legal fees and buying out the minority shareholders, the amount of money left for packaging, new lines, cashflow etc. was minimal. I knew in my very core that we'd done the wrong deal.

We weren't in the right 'head-space' to make such huge decisions; we were too stressed. A very good friend of mine (at this time in my life I had yet to meet him), Croz Crossley, The Mindset Technician, talks about this a lot. People under stress and pressure only make bad decisions. How right is he.

Claire's Diamond

You always have a choice. Even when you think you don't, you do – you just have to find it and have the courage to take it.

Both John and I dealt with this in our different ways, and in fact didn't really speak to each other about this until a long time afterwards. He thought I was ok with it; I thought he was ok with it. The rot had set in though.

John had been struggling for some time with the stress of the business. I knew this, but there was nothing I could do. It wasn't an easy time for me either. Different people deal with stress in different ways. I have a very high threshold.

I can remain tenacious, resilient and determined even through seemingly impossible times. Lots of reasons for that: my upbringing, surviving my blood clot, carrying on through all the hard times and having a deep knowing that I will come out the other side, and a deep belief in myself, my abilities and my destiny of success.

John, on the other hand, wasn't dealing with it in the same way. Alcohol was his coping mechanism. He spiralled into a deep dark place which resulted in a breakdown. This was a difficult time for all of us. It hit the kids, the business, and I had to keep even more plates spinning. Alcohol dependency is evil; it ruins lives.

I am sure you can see a pattern forming here: when something really bad happened, there was a high for me to lean on, to pull me through. It's almost as though someone up there was saying to me 'Hang on in there, it'll come good'. Well this high came in the shape of an invitation as a food entrepreneur to St James's Palace. Me... invited to St James's Palace!

The determination for me to change the wrong foot I got off on in Partridges rewarded me more than I could have ever imagined. It was the buyer at

Claire's Diamond

Even when things are at their worst, if you can somehow stay positive life meets you half way and brings a helping hand.

Partridges who put my name forward when asked for recommendations for some food and drink entrepreneurs to attend the Palace for an event.

I now have the invitation in a frame at home. I ended up being invited twice. I couldn't believe it. In three short but long years from launching, I was stood in St James's Palace, sipping on royal champagne in a room full of top weight business people, celebrities and royalty. How surreal, extremely surreal indeed.

Just as had happened to me numerous times now, a moment of serendipity was never far away. At the Palace there were a few:

- Words of wisdom from a perfect stranger
- Meeting Peter Jones for the third time!
- Meeting a kind gentleman would help me more than I ever could've imagined

At St James's Palace, in one of the staterooms, I chatted throughout the evening in the company of the most energising, intelligent and uplifting group of people I have ever had the privilege of being in a room with. One of those was a perfect stranger who said these words of wisdom to me: **'Don't sell your soul'.**

I tend to wear my heart on my sleeve, very open; I don't tend to hold much back. So, when someone asks me something, on occasion they can get more than they bargained for. This occasion was the stranger at the Palace. I don't know his name, but he was a very influential person; they all were. He had a calm knowing about him.

He asked how things were going, how was the business etc. I was honest; I told him about the struggles we'd been and still were going through. He reached out with both his hands to hold mine, and that's when he said, **'Don't sell your soul'.**

I didn't understand the full meaning behind what he was saying at first. You see at this point in my life all I was thinking about was share values, sales, money, investors etc.

I was literally running on auto pilot keeping everything going. His words stopped me in my tracks though, kind of re-wired me back to the Claire I knew I was deep down and had almost lost, the one who wasn't on the run, governed by stress, slowly losing herself.

What I later realised was that it wasn't about money or shares and equity. It was about self-worth, self-respect and what I have shared earlier about knowing when to stand up to life and not be beaten down.

To know when enough is enough. It was too late though. With this clarity and knowing our actions with our investors, I knew I had already sold my soul.

When I arrived at the Palace I looked down the guest list, and whose name should be there alongside all the other top weight people? Peter Jones! My stomach did a flip.

The first time I met Peter, I was 'stalking' him. The second time he told me that I had a dream, a business, but was broke. Now I was potentially going to meet him again.

I decided to make a point of meeting him. I needed to put that ghost to bed. It took a lot of picking myself up after *Dragons' Den*, and I saw this as a way to do just that. I clocked him across the room and went over to him. He was talking to celebrity chef Heston Blumenthal, so I waited for the right moment then started to talk to him.

He remembered me from the Den, and asked how I was, and I had my photo taken with him. I was thinking back to the MADE Festival, and to the Den. Now here I was rubbing shoulders with all these people in St James's Palace, and talking to Peter Jones, the man whom years earlier I was running around a hotel trying to get to speak to. Yes, I wasn't in clover, but my business was  still alive and fighting to live another day, and that would do for now.

My third serendipitous moment at the Palace was to meet a gentleman called Will King, the founder of King of Shaves, and one of the UK's best-known entrepreneurs. Will has helped me since, advising and mentoring me. Will asked me how things were, and as before with others, I was honest with him. Will agreed with me: our deal with the investors wasn't good. Had I not met Will that day I don't know what I would've done; his help and support got me through some of my very darkest times.

At one moment in the Palace amongst all of this going on, I found myself stood, on my own, with the Duke and Duchess of York, yep, just me in a conversation with them. I recall thinking this is too weird, amazing but weird... I am stood in St James's Palace, glass of champagne in one hand, and using my other hand to talk with (as I always do!), with royalty. You couldn't make it up, could you!

I was cracking on with things, taking care of business. The Waitrose listing went live. I was as proud as punch stood there that day with both the lines on the shelves. Remember I said that behind every brand there is a story. Well there you go, I bet you didn't imagine just how much of a story there can be behind a brand. So, what now?

The Practical Stuff

Yay – you're now on the last step of my 8 steps. This last step seems simple, but sometimes it's elusive and pressure seems to squeeze it out of you. It can also be counterintuitive, but trust me, don't neglect it.

STEP 8:
Have Fun (No really... You must. If the fun goes the passion follows.)

You've invested months, most probably years, to get to this point, and will have made countless sacrifices on all levels: financially, time spent on your passion and dream away from family and friends, sleepless nights; you know what I'm talking about as you will have done all of this to have got to this last stage.

It's damned hard work to get to this point, so huge congratulations to you for your faith, determination and belief to get to the point where your hard work and hustle has come to fruition and you are ready to launch your baby to the world.

There is even harder work to come... but always remember to have fun, be creative, follow your gut, keep your passion alive, and always remember why you started your food business in the first place. Hold onto the feeling of what inspired you from the off, and don't ever let that go.

Real Account

HOW I'VE HELPED AND
WORKED WITH A FOOD BUSINESS

Hello, I'm Barbara Bray, the director of a technical services and nutrition consultancy, Alo Solutions Ltd, which provides food safety and nutritional labelling advice, development and training to food industry clients and fresh produce growers.

In October 2016 I was awarded a Nuffield Farming Scholarship. The award requires a minimum of eight weeks of international travel to be carried out as part of the research over an 18-month period.

I had four weeks until the deadline to submit my final travel plan. There was an additional Global Focus programme visiting six countries in seven weeks as part of a group of scholars from around the world to study farming and food production plus the compulsory international conference held in Brasilia for a week!

How would I plan to be out of my business for 16 weeks of one year?

How would I approach my clients, organise my budget and manage family commitments?

It was at this point that I realised I would need support to produce my project plan, to secure my client pipeline and protect my revenue stream. I turned to LinkedIn as my usual port of call to find people and whilst scrolling through various articles, I read a post which mentioned Claire Brumby, The Food Guide.

I instantly warmed to her profile as a mentor, entrepreneur and creative professional but was apprehensive about whether she would consider a non-food production business as a client... I gave her a call.

I explained my business, my project and that I had a deadline to submit my project plan to the Nuffield Farming Trust and we put a date for a half-day planning session in the diary.

I instantly liked Claire's approach. She helped me to visualise what 'good' looked like throughout the 18-month journey that I would take. For example, how to prioritise the different challenges such as finding subcontractors and ensuring continuity of work, then break these activities down into bite sized pieces.

I found her story of setting up her business, and her journey as an entrepreneur, inspirational and motivating. Most of all I felt an overall sense of calm. The project plan was done; I had a strategy in place to manage my workload, new clients, Nuffield travel and research.

As the months sped by I was able to modify the plan as my situation changed and I scheduled my Skype calls with Claire around my travels. By February, I had a Nuffield mentor but I needed Claire to keep me pointing in the right direction for my business.

She reminded me to keep looking for new clients and new business associates which resulted in winning bigger and interesting contracts. She helped me focus on the core goal and helped me to decide which things I would have to sacrifice within my business to sustain it throughout the scholarship period.

I have days when I feel like I am winning but, on the days when I don't feel like that, Claire's advice has been invaluable.

Barbara Bray
www.alo-solutions.com

What Would Claire Do Now?

The deal with the investors was wrong. We had jumped out of the frying pan into the fire in terms of where we led ourselves from a cashflow perspective. When I advise my clients now with questions they have around funding I always ask so many deep questions about where they are at:

- What are sales like?
- Are there any external strains on the cashflow or with the business?
- When do you think you need cash by?
- What do you need it for?
- Can we make any changes in the business overheads?

In the early stages of their business life, many entrepreneurs hawk off small amounts of equity in return for services. I have recently had a client come to me with this. The lady in question was going to give quite a good proportion of shares in return for some consultancy work. It gets messy, and in my opinion won't end well, so I would not advise this.

I'd like to endorse the advice I was given about 'not selling your soul'. If it feels wrong don't do it.

In my heart I knew that the deal we did was fundamentally wrong. I remember the feeling sat at my desk when it had gone through, and there and then in that very moment I no longer felt like my business was my own. It's almost as if in a second it died.

I was in the midst of what I like to think of as a culture clash. I am entrepreneurial through and through, and to a degree felt like my wings had been clipped. I felt like I couldn't be me in the culture of the business that was evolving. I would advise you to always remain true to you; when you don't you can't operate in life let alone in your business.

Claire's Diamond

You can't outrun the truth. It's impossible... it will always catch you.

CHAPTER 8

When the Fun Goes the Passion Dies

We'd been working and growing the business with our investors. John still wasn't in a good place. We'd introduced five more bags of crisps to our range, and sales were increasing, but the profits weren't. The business was growing but not fast enough.

I think you can feel through my words as I am writing this part that the fun, passion and drive was waning.

I was deeply unhappy. I felt I was on the very hamster wheel I had been fortunate enough to be plucked off at the very beginning of this roller coaster. What was it all for?

The fun and passion had gone from the business. I felt like I was working alone, and unsupported in the business from all angles. If this was all it had come to, then I wasn't sure it was what I wanted.

We would have monthly board meetings with the investors; by this time we were a board of five. The rot

Claire's Diamond

Is where you've arrived where you planned to be? If not, you must make a change.

which had set in 18 months ago continued to grow. I reflected on what I'd set out to do, and what I'd achieved:

- Launch a healthier snacking brand ✓
- Win awards for the brand ✓
- List with major retailers ✓
- Make a difference to people through healthier eating ✓
- I'd had fun along the way ✓
- The kids learned so much ✓
- I met some amazing people, made new friends ✓
- I learned through experience that which no amount of money could ever buy ✓
- Made some of my happiest memories which will stay with me forever ✓
- Became an expert in the field of launching and growing a food business ✓

I'd achieved all I'd set out to do. The only thing I wasn't was massively wealthy. When I look back though the wealth aspect wasn't a key driver for me. Perhaps it should have been? Perhaps I should have been more money driven from the off?

What I did know was that right now no amount of money in the world would make me happy. My family was suffering and at the heart of that suffering was this business. I'd made a promise to myself years ago: that I'd never let stress drive me to that ill place I'd once been. I felt like I'd let myself down and fallen into that trap so many of us do: live to work, not work to live.

Now I'm not advocating an easy life, or not working hard. Far from it. I would guess you know having read this far that I'm not one to shy away from working hard. There is a tipping point though. Be aware of yours.

John and I decided we wanted to sell our shares. We'd lost our passion for the business. It had been an exhausting journey. We'd had all the pre-launch years trying to get the business off the ground, launch the brand. Then once we'd achieved that, it had been relentless month on month, year on year. I had nothing left to give.

I was stuck between a rock and hard place. Scrubbys was like a baby, but I knew in my heart it was time to let it go for it to grow. We called a board meeting, and a full decision was made to go for a sale. I created a full memorandum of information about the business to present to prospective buyers.

We ran a sale process for several months which brought a good couple of offers for the business, but

Claire's Diamond

Ask for help. It's not a
weakness. It's a display of the
biggest strength by having
the courage to reach out,
ask for and receive help.

for one reason or another the final detail couldn't be agreed with the prospective purchaser and the board.

The relationships between the board members had reached an irretrievable position by this stage, so an administration process was entered. I knew there was value in the brand, so I set about meeting interested parties to sell the brand, to take it to a safe destination where I was confident it would grow and thrive.

I had a meeting arranged with a gentleman in Manchester at The Lowry Hotel. I recall driving there and thinking I just wanted to get this all resolved now. I'd mentally already left the business, but I wanted a safe pair of hands for the brand. It was a funny feeling: I still had passion for the brand, and I am still to this day an extremely proud founder and brand ambassador. What I no longer had was that fire in my belly and the same feeling. It had taken so much; it had in fact taken everything.

The meeting went very well. We immediately got on, and I felt I'd be happy if he was to become the new owner of Scrubbys. I shared the story of how and why Scrubbys began. It was quite nice in one sense. When you're at the coal face in the thick of something day in day out for so long you can, and we almost all do, forget or neglect to step back and see how far you've come. This was one of those lessons.

He was very complimentary about what we had achieved in the space of time, and how little the brand and business had cost in relation to what he knew it should and does cost in this fiercely competitive category to make a dent, and we had certainly done that.

Not many days after that meeting a deal was agreed. AIB Foods in Wolverhampton were to be the new owners of the Scrubbys brand.

I worked with them for a few months to carry out a thorough handover. During this process I knew I'd done the right thing, and that they were the right people to grow the brand.

I wasn't wrong; they have extended the range to now include Quinoa, Lentil and Hummus Crisps. When we sold the brand, the range was seven bags of crisps. At the time of writing this they have a 30-plus range of bags, new lines and sell to in excess of 21 countries.

Claire's Diamond

Everybody wants to be a diamond, but few are willing to get cut. What do I mean by that? Hard work is what.

Onwards and Upwards, Leaping Again

Remember back in the first chapter I said that I'd had a gradual awakening and wasn't quite sure what to do with it? My food entrepreneur journey helped me get greater clarity on this.

Hard work is getting off your arse when you really don't feel like it. Getting up the eighth time when you've been knocked down seven. That's the reason for the diamond in my logo. I was a chunk of coal back when all this started; I've taken so many knocks, had the cuts, been shaped. Still tons to learn; it never stops, and that's what's exciting.

I am not the same person I was when I started this food journey, and I'm not the same person I was when we sold the brand, and I am pretty sure by the time you read this book I will be a different, better version of myself too.

Isn't that what we all hope for? I guess so, otherwise you wouldn't be reading this book, wanting to learn through my experience.

Just think with every knock, every cut, every setback, you are being moulded into your own beautiful diamond.

It takes courage, guts, determination, blind faith and self-belief, but remember what Muhammad Ali said: **'If my mind can conceive it, and my heart can believe it, then I can achieve it'**.

Claire's Diamond

Plough your own furrow; don't be dictated into something when you have a belief that you can achieve so much more.

What I'd learnt about myself was that I wanted to use all I'd gained through my experience to become the mentor and consultant that I once so desperately needed. Back to what I learnt about myself from my double glazing days, that I was a people person. How was I going to get myself out there in this vein though?

At first, I was very lost, although I wanted to sell the brand, and it was the right thing to do. Waking up one morning and it no longer being there was hard. I didn't know what to do, how to 'be' anymore.

Every day for years all my time, actions, focus, attention, everything had been about Scrubbys. Now it wasn't there. Not to mention that I needed to start earning money.

I knew people were interested in the journey. I had been public speaking for years now, telling the story, inspiring others on their journey, talking to established food businesses about how they can grow, and motivating other would-be entrepreneurs to 'take the leap', and I absolutely love to do this. If in any of my talks I can help, inspire or motivate just one person I am extremely happy.

I hadn't had any speaking training though and knew this was going to be a key tool in my skillset and services going forward, and one which I wanted to do more of (and thankfully am now).

So, I decided to investigate how to do this. I came across a 'Be a Better Speaker' event hosted by Brad Burton – The UK's #1 Motivational Business Speaker. I'd heard of Brad, and boy am I glad I met him. He's one of the most genuine people I have ever had the good fortune to meet. Look him up.

He had an event running the next day, and as chance would have it someone had dropped out last minute so there was a place available. Serendipity looking out for me again. There have been so many *Sliding Door* moments for me over the years, and this was most definitely one of them.

It's all down to how open you are to the chances coming your way though. The same two people could have the very same opportunities presented to them. Knowing what to do with them is an entirely different thing, and something which I think we all need to work on for ourselves.

How do you know which to take, what to look out for?

- You need to know yourself.
- Know your why.
- Know where you want to go.
- Have a pretty good idea on how you're going to get there.

That event really got me locked in and focused on my next steps. It's also where I met Croz Crossley. He helped me in bringing The Food Guide to life and in programming my brain from feeling lost to ready and prepared for success on the next stages of my journey.

He's a fabulous teacher and mentor. Without Brad and Croz entering my life at the time they did I would've had a much rockier transition from Scrubbys founder to becoming The Food Guide. I am extremely grateful to them both.

Well, just as I had deployed good old guerrilla tactics with Scrubbys and the advice from Wilfred Emmanuel-Jones about being a disruptive influence, it was now time to turn them on again.

One night I was scrolling through Twitter when an image of a lady lying on the floor surrounded by packets of crisps caught my eye. That lady was the English model Iskra Lawrence. She is also a National Eating Disorders Association (NEDA) brand ambassador and creator of the NEDA Inspires Award.

The crisps were Seabrook's, and it was a fabulous PR stunt opportunity. I emailed the CEO (who I'd met in the Scrubbys days), sent him the picture and told him what a good idea I thought him doing something with it would be.

The reason for Iskra doing the photo was to hit back at critics calling her fat. She was hitting back at negativity, showing her true grit, determination, ambition and unfaltering tenacity for her beliefs. This got me thinking, many things... amongst them why this attitude is what you need in business:

True Grit, Determination, Ambition, Tenacity, Resilience and Self-Belief

I then thought, hang about, I can do this! As the founder of Scrubbys Vegetable Crisps I can do the same. What a fabulous way to get some attention for my new business launch. What an amazing way to get my guerrilla on!

I knew I had to act fast otherwise I'd miss the moment, so texted a local photographer I knew. I sent her the picture and asked if we could create the same shot, but with me and Scrubbys. Yes, she was up for it. I arranged to meet her the next morning. I went along to her studio with John and my eldest daughter. As you can see in the picture, that's just what I did!

This took me out of my comfort zone, at the time a 42-year-old mum of three, well out of it! However, on reflection that's nothing new to what's happened over the Scrubbys journey years when inventing, creating and bringing the brand to life.

The picture also symbolised the process of the brand's life. It really did 'strip me bare'. It took everything: physically, emotionally, financially and mentally. I am sure this will resonate with anybody who has done this, particularly women who have the added challenge of raising a family.

I later discovered that Iskra was born in Wolverhampton; how funny that one chapter of my life closed there with the new owners of Scrubbys. The next opening:

Claire's Diamond

I firmly believe what's meant for you won't pass you by.

launching my new business using guerrilla through an idea inspired by someone born there – anyway I digress.

The result of this guerrilla action was that my new business was well and truly launched. I tweeted Iskra with the image and she put it out on her Instagram and Twitter feeds; this reached over two million people.

I contacted my local press, told them about my new business venture, and supplied the picture; yes, you guessed it, just as before I made the front page. I was back!

When the shit is hitting the fan, as it will, because that's just how life is, I believe you need to have faith and trust that all is happening in perfect timing for the right reasons for what you need, good and bad. It's only when you look back that you are able to join the dots of the 'whys'.

That's good and bad, by the way: ride the good times, knuckle down and learn in the bad, turn them into good by taking what you've learnt and using that going forward.

On your food business journey, I feel sure that you will encounter many occasions which will mirror situations like I've faced. We all do. There will undoubtedly be painful times, but pain is good... it's an indication that you've outgrown where you are, and it pushes you to grow. If you weren't feeling the pain, you wouldn't be ready. Accepting this is hard, but it's what will take you from your comfort zone on the path to realising your potential.

One of the key attributes I think you need as a food business founder is resilience, but what does it mean? It's the measure of how you cope when things are shit, not how you cope when they are going well. When life pushes you, push back harder, get harder, don't give in, and never ever give up.

I believe as food business founders we have all the ingredients for our own success. Don't seek or rely on anyone to bring you the ingredients for your success. You and you alone can do this because you already have them within you, though you often need someone like me to help with the way you use them, and in which order.

What Would Claire Do Now?

Because I was running on empty, I'd become mentally weak. I was susceptible to being pushed around. I wasn't at times as strong as I know I can be, or indeed am. Certain aspects I look back on and I can't believe I, ME stood for it. You must always stand up for yourself; don't let yourself be bullied. Don't ever let anyone dictate your worth. The minute they try you are worth more.

Look after yourself; you are no good to anyone, least of all yourself and your business, if you are running on empty. You can only go at 100mph for so long. Trust me on this one; I am 100% right.

The decision made to sell was the right one. There is nothing that I would do differently at this stage. The brand found its safe pair of hands and is growing and thriving. I learnt so much on the journey which enables me to give THE best advice to my clients, not just from a textbook but from the heart with passion, from real experience.

This is worth its weight. I know the exact pain, difficulties, challenges, circumstances, predicaments and mental space each of my clients are at when they come to me.

It could be a manufacturing question, it could be about raising investment, routes to market, pitching to retailers, strategies to grow, or an exit plan, or even from the very off how to even launch. I have knowledge, experience and proven expertise to be that mentor and consultant in your business.

Had I not done all I did on my own journey I wouldn't be in this expert position I am in, which I am enormously grateful to be. The challenges we started with were a huge contributory factor throughout. Fundamentally, we launched with too little cash. We took on a huge category without enough back-up. You can't run away from anything. If you do it will eventually catch you up. This factor caught us up. We were on the back foot.

Essentially, we were ahead of the curve, ahead of our time. We were pioneers for healthy snacking, and the general masses weren't quite there, so sales took far too long to achieve, and we didn't have the cashflow for the time it would take to gain the momentum.

Claire's Diamond

Experience is the best teacher and education.

What Could I Do for You?

I hope you've enjoyed all you've read as you've got to this point. I'm sure you'll agree that my journey was a rollercoaster and then some!

Yours doesn't have to be quite so fraught though, and I hope there's information and advice in here which lives up to the promise at the beginning of the book, and you've taken something away to help you as you reach to achieve your entrepreneurial dreams.

If you'd like to book me as your business speaker at your next event or host a masterclass, I cover topics which include;

- How to Launch a Food Business
- Branding
- Marketing
- Routes to Market
- Pitching to Buyers
- Women in Business
- Embracing Change
- Working Outside Your Comfort Zone
- Work Life Balance
- Starting a Business with No Knowledge/ Experience in the Sector
- Success and Failure
- Launching and Building a Brand
- Guerrilla Marketing

If you'd like to know more about how I can directly help you in your business, and this can be in several ways, and can be as much or as little as is required, please do get in touch.

Or I can help from a distance in the case of my mentoring or coaching packages which can be found on my website under mentoring and coaching.

I can personally help with all, but am not limited to, the following:

- Business development/strategy planning sessions
- Immediate, medium and longer-term planning for the business and brand, to include if desired full operational laser-focused business plan to assist with launch or growth and map out next steps. Ongoing support and assistance if required to implement the agreed plan and adjust as necessary.
- Launch planning
- New lines, range extensions etc.
- Retailer strategy, pitching and presentation
- Key account management if required. I have successfully listed clients with major retailers: Tesco, Waitrose, Ocado, Co-op, Sainsbury's, WHS, Asda etc. and have experience in working with retailer portals and systems.
- Marketing strategy – for brand activation and implementation
- Project and interim management
- Marketing planning and campaign management
- Show and event exhibition planning and representation, both consumer and trade
- Stand development and support in managing of events

- Sales
- Identifying and mapping targets and prospects, both retailer and wholesale
- Establishing routes to market
- Full sales representation if required
- In summary I can provide a full support package, or individual tailored services. I have a strong influential network which I can merge services from; these include however aren't restricted to:
  - Website and social media
  - Product branding
  - Packaging design and sourcing
  - Photography
  - Finance and funding
  - Manufacturing partners
  - Logistics, warehousing and distribution

Whichever route, my mission is simple... to help your business and brand grow and thrive profitably through sharing the wealth of expertise, knowledge and contacts I have gained over the years.

If you'd like to reach out to me, I'd love to hear from you, and how you're doing in your business.

If you'd like to know more about how I can help you, more information can be found at www.clairebrumby.com

Please join me over on Twitter, Instagram and Facebook @theclairebrumby. I'd also love to welcome you into my FREE Facebook Group: The Entrepreneur Coach. I'm in there every day, and live every week sharing lots of great stuff with all the members, would be great to have you in there too.

You can contact me at hello@clairebrumby.com.

I look forward to hearing from you.

If you're going to launch your business, DO IT.

If you're facing challenges in your business, YOU CAN get through them... find a way.

Now go build that business of your dreams.

Always CHOOSE LIFE, and most importantly BE HAPPY!

CHAPTER 9

Valuable Bites: The Icing on the Cake!

Ok, so I hope you've read the book and arrived here in that way, but if you're just jumping in at the back here, this is where you'll find those 'top tips and valuable bits' I mentioned. I believe these will be of amazing help. Keep this book on your desk next to your laptop for the next time:

- You get an email from a buyer.
- You're about to embark on a trade show or set off to sell your wares at a festival.
- You're feeling a bit low (we all have those days!).

You should find something in this chapter to save you some or all of these:

- Time
- Money
- Sanity

How to never give up as an entrepreneur

1. Look after yourself – your health is your first wealth, so look after it

This includes mental health as well as physical health. To avoid burnout, make time to look after these. For me this is through open water swimming; in fact, when you read this I will be a successful channel relay swimmer – who knows, maybe my next book will be about that?!

Any type of physical exercise will make you feel so much better, and more able to cope.

A healthy body and healthy mind are the underpinning to all you will achieve; it's non-negotiable.

2. Lower your expectations

Tim Ferriss was turned down 25 times before he could find someone to publish his bestseller, *The 4-Hour Work Week*.

How many times do we see seemingly 'overnight' successes? Yes, they're all around.

Although actually they're not... success takes a lot of time.

There are no quick fixes; be prepared to put the time in.

Success will not come to you overnight.

3. Stay strong – you are stronger than you think

How many of us can look back now to situations we thought we were never going to get through?

I am guessing each and every one of us, yes? Well then, there you go, you know you're stronger than you sometimes think – you just needed me to remind you.

Recall those thoughts and feelings when you are not feeling too strong. You'll be reminded of your positive track record of getting through tough times.

4. Action – never stop taking action; persistence wins the day

Please, please, please do not be one of those people who reads this book, or who goes to a seminar, who goes to that event, becomes all fired up and does... NOTHING.

Yes, a big, fat, zero nothing. Why? Fear? Lack of discipline? Can't be arsed?

Fear is a killer. It's also an illusion. I believe it's the biggest fuel to procrastination. Different people have different levels and perceptions of fear. We have most probably heard these:

Face **E**verything **A**nd **R**ise
Face **E**verything **A**nd **R**un

I prefer

Fuck **E**verything **A**nd **R**oar

Whatever excuse you give yourself it will be just that. An excuse. Stop talking about it. If you're doing it... DO IT.

Whatever it is you want to do. Just do it and keep doing it.

5. Fake it until you make it – it's OK to fake success before you get there

I think we all have done or do this to a certain extent. That's ok though. How are you going to get there if you don't know where you are going?

For me certainly, in my early Scrubbys days a lot of progression and momentum was gained though this very action.

6. Stay focused – don't look back, left or right, or at your competitors; keep your eye on your own goal

Another trap which I am certain we can all fall into. Do not, I repeat do not, look at what others/your competitors are doing. Firstly, they may be faking it, so what you're seeing isn't real anyway!

Secondly you have no idea where they are on their own journey; they may have been slogging at it far longer than you even know.

Thirdly, I compare this to when I am in a lane swimming. The minute I glance to my left or to my right my stroke suffers. When it suffers I slow down. Fact.

Nothing my competitor did slowed me down. It was my own action of looking left or right, not focusing on my own lane, which slowed me down. Do not do this in your business or life. Keep your eye on your goal. Keep YOUR focus.

7. The wall – just before the corner turns you hit the wall

Life and business have a funny way of doing this. You can see the end in sight. Your goal is just beyond your reach, then something totally unexpected or unprepared for comes in and curveballs you. Think back to your staying strong moments. It's just another one of these, and it will pass.

8. Your goal – yes!

Now this could be a big goal, or a small goal. These eight stages can come (as I'm sure you know) every day in the life of an entrepreneur in their business. But deep down isn't that what we like? The buzz, the thrill, the opportunity and the ability to move and shift as we see fit to take us where we want to go.

Here's some top tips for when you're trading at markets and food festivals

Mark your space out in chalk on your patio/ drive, garage floor etc.

Or get some tape and mark the space out on your carpet in your dining room/lounge. Have a play around with how your stand will go, move your banners/table around and get a better idea on what will flow best and work best for the show. If you are trading from there, i.e. at a show/festival, it may be best in a different way than if it's a trade show for example.

Invest in some rubber soled Wellies and stand on cardboard (to keep your feet warm)

A few heat patches on your back don't go amiss too; they prevent you getting excruciating back ache!

Don't write an event off before it's even started

I remember vividly various markets and festivals when the heavens opened to torrential rain. Your customers are getting soaked too, and the last thing they want is a miserable trader, so get your smile on... a smile and positivity can go a long way to convincing people to buy.

If you're unsure on whether to exhibit at a given show/festival.

Have a look at the exhibitor list from the previous year and contact some of the exhibitors. They will usually share with you if it was good or not.

It's not all about making a huge profit at these shows and markets

Yes, always aim to cover your costs, including your time. That said, the benefits can be more far reaching than you can ever plan for, to be honest, though. You never quite know. If we'd not done Carfest I wouldn't have the Chris Evans picture. That led to national coverage in the newspaper and a local radio show. I know that is an extreme example, and you don't have that chance at all shows. I do know though that without question at every single event we picked up an additional farm shop/deli listing or were able to use the event to direct consumers to whichever listing we wanted to support.

Which brings me nicely on to prepare, prepare, prepare

By failing to prepare, you are preparing to fail. Why are you attending the show/fair? Is it to increase sales? Is it to direct to a listing? Is it to promote a new product? Is it to build a mailing list? Can you do additional market research for some NPD (New Product Development) you are undertaking? Without a doubt there are always multiple wins to be gained if you think your event through and thoroughly prepare.

The preparation also extends to the weather

Have clothes for all eventualities if you are outdoors. A pack-a-mac isn't sexy but is worth its weight! Preparation extends to doing your homework on what stock to take too. Find out the expected footfall and plan your stock appropriately.

Cashflow

Some start-ups overlook the cashflow which weekly markets/festivals can add to your business. In our very early days we relied on that coming in through being at these shows. When you add up over the year what you have turned over at these events it's not to be sniffed at. These are great places for stock rotation too; use the shortest shelf-dated stock first as your stockists need the longest dated stock.

Added opportunities?

I remember one summer it was scorchio and we knew from experience that bottles of water at this particular event we were due to trade at were extortionate, I mean like £3+ for a 250ml bottle. We went to our local cash 'n carry the day before and bought a load of bottles of water. We sold a combo of crisps and water for a fab price. We made extra sales, and word got around that we were also selling cheaper water, so we were extremely busy. We sold out of crisps and water. That's what all traders want: an empty van at the end of the day.

Keep reviewing which you attend and keep a look out for any new ones

Make sure you are fishing in the right pond; know where your customers are hanging out.

You can never have too many tarpaulins or sheets

These are fab for wind breaks and waterproofing.

Fully equip your trader's toolkit

Cling film, bungy ropes, mini blackboards, rope, string, tape, liquid chalk pens, Blu Tack, Sellotape, pens, business cards, surface cleaner for black boards, cloth to wipe boards and stall with, carrier bags (just in case), platform trolley for wheeling stock about, big plastic containers to decant your stock into (cardboard cases get soaked = damaged stock).

Cash float

The simpler your pricing structure = the simpler your float requirements. Don't underestimate the amount of change you will need, especially at the start of the event when every one of your customers will have a £20 note. £1 coins and £5 notes are your essentials.

Enjoy yourself!

Seriously there is some fun to be had from these events. You're there for the duration, so make the best of it and enjoy yourself.

Top tips for exhibiting at trade shows

- If you don't think you can afford to exhibit at a show independently contact your local Chamber of Commerce; they may have a food division with a presence at the show. In the case of Scrubbys this was Select Lincolnshire. For the first two years we went along with them and a handful of other brands, and this was the difference in us being able to exhibit at shows such as Speciality & Fine Food Fair.

- Really think about the space you need; you can get away with a smaller space than you think. Certainly in your start-up/early days.

- This sounds daft, but remember you are there to meet buyers; it's not the same as when you're at a festival, market or food fair. Adapt your approach accordingly.

- A lot of these events have a meet the buyer option. Contact each show well in advance so you are able to take up every opportunity.

- If you can, book early so you make full use of the fee you pay by being included in the show catalogue and marketing.

- Make friends with other businesses going; to keep costs down on accommodation you can maybe hire an Airbnb together.

- Don't pounce on buyers. Again, sounds daft, but I have been that eager, passionate brand owner, keen and desperate for the listing. Play it cool; it works so much better.

- Talk to the buyer's face, not their name badge, whilst you're clocking where they are from. This is a pet hate they have.

- Make full use of your event space – this includes the height. Can you use banners, branded bunting etc?

- Don't sit down looking at your phone or reading a paper whilst drinking coffee and eating a bacon butty at your stand. This may sound obvious, but there are countless times I've been at shows and the exhibitors have complained they're quiet, when in fact they've not been working the show at all.

- Keep all your refreshments out of view, don't eat on your stand and have plenty of water accessible. Dehydration at these shows is a killer. Oh, and wear flat shoes!

- Have your tool kit ready. For some reason everyone forgets the stapler, and you always need one. Other good essentials are: scissors, Blu Tack, pens, notebook, iPad, bin, wipes.

- Keep your samples fresh and your counter clean.

- Find the # hashtag for the event on social media and jump on that in the lead-up to and during the show, inviting people to come and visit your stand.

- Capture all details of everyone you speak to on your stand with good old-fashioned pen and paper, so go armed with a clipboard and lined paper.

- You will speak to so many people, so make a note whilst your conversation is fresh in your mind; you can then personalise your follow-up communication better.

- Follow up! It's shocking how many people forget to follow up or leave the follow-up too late. Ideally follow up in the same week.

Top tips for approaching, pitching and listing with a multiple/retailer buyer

- It's a marathon, not a sprint – it can take an age to track the right one down.

- There are no hard and fast rules on how to – just find what suits you best.

- They move around; be prepared to just get through a door and the buyer changes.

- Make LinkedIn and Google your best friend; it's surprising how you can track buyers down.

- Know the business of the buyer you're pitching to and demonstrate also that you understand your consumer, but keep things concise.

- Ask when their category reviews and listing windows are and if there are any mid-window opportunities.

- Don't pin your cashflow around these listings; always have revenue coming in from other routes to market.

- Be patient and persistent, although avoid Mondays when trying to contact them.

- Adapt your pitch to the buyer, i.e. what worked for you with an independent buyer won't necessarily work with a retailer buyer.

- Remember they're just human!

- Let your passion shine through, but equally don't be blinded by it.

- Reverse engineer your sell – i.e. put yourself in their shoes.
  - Sell why they should list you.
  - Explain what's in it for them, their category.
  - How will you enhance/grow their category?
  - What is the benefit to listing your product?

- Don't take rejection personally; move on to your next target. You need thick skin in this game.

- Hit it hard from the off. If your products don't perform well in the first 12 weeks you're in danger of a de-list.

- Go into your local store once listed; chat with the shelf stackers about your product – they often give you some gold nuggets to take back to your buyer.

- You'll be rated going forward on how many units you sell per store per week – get to know and understand these numbers.

- If you are not performing to these, ask how long you have to rectify, then do all you can to drive customers to buy from those stores.

10 Top tips for approaching and working with independent buyers — farm shops/delis etc.

- There is a high likelihood that you will be talking to/approaching the owner of the shop/ deli, therefore it's their own money they are investing. This pitch is one where you can, most definitely, let your passion shine through.

- The provenance of your ingredients and product will be of great interest to them, more so (as a rule) than with the multiple buyers, so this should and needs to be a huge part of the conversation.

- Do not try and phone/visit them across their peak times which will be around lunchtime.

- Visit the shop in advance of approaching them; have a clear idea on where you think your product will fit in, and understand what they already have in your products category.

- Once you have your products on their shelves, nurture the listing:

  - Offer to go in and sample in store (edible marketing)

  - Run some promotions/offers

- If you attend a farmer's market or food festival near the shop, direct customers from the market to buy again from the shop. Equally when you have a stand at a farmer's market or festival and have customers buying your products, ask them where they shop locally; you can then go to that shop and share that you sold lots at the event and start a conversation about getting listed with them.

- When you are in the shop sampling, offer to go in early and brief the staff about your product – they will welcome this, and you then have staff armed with knowledge about your products when you aren't there to sell them.

- Don't be afraid to ring for repeat orders – give it time for the initial order to sell, but don't think you are bothering them by ringing; you're not. They may just be too busy to contact you. You will be helping them.

- Often, they will hold 'Meet the Supplier' event days for their customers; always attend these, because people love to meet the producer.

- These types of shops are filled with award winning products; once you've entered and won awards, make sure you shout about them to these buyers.

- Target some of the top 50 farm shops and delis in the UK. When you are stocked by some of them use your sales data to help when talking to other targets.

- Regularly use your social media to support them; follow the shop accounts and tweet/blog/promote the fact that they stock your products.

Here's my top 10 business tips, what I have learned along the way

1. Don't try and go it alone; it won't work.

2. Let people underestimate you – never underestimate them.

3. Sales are key – neglect these and you'll fold.

4. Ask questions, lots of them, and listen – but be prepared to take the answers and actions on board.

5. But... ask the right people the right questions.

6. Listen to your body otherwise you'll burn out – this is both in a mental and physical sense.

7. Play to your strengths – reach out for help on your weaknesses.

8. It's going to take longer than you think or want to get where you want to be – have patience.

9. Do stuff, take action – you can't plough a field by thinking about it.

10. Have fun, be passionate and enjoy the ride – if you're not you're on the wrong one.

De-mything some of the acronyms

(I wish I'd known some of these back in the day)

ASN
Advanced Shipping Notification: detailed shipment information that is sent electronically from the shipper to a customer in advance of the delivery.

BACKHAUL
The reverse logistics or return journey after a delivery has taken place. An example would be the return journey from dropping off stock at a retailer's back to the warehouse.

BARKER CARDS
The cards which sit on the shelf of the retailer with the price of your product on them. When you are on promotion, with some retailers you have to pay a fee towards the barker card to have your promo price on it.

BB
Best before date

BOGSHP
Buy one get second half price

BOP
Back of pack information on the back of your packaging.

BRC

The British Retail Consortium, which is the leading trade association for UK retailing. Although the BRC food safety standard began in the UK, it is now recognised as a global standard. There are over 17,000 BRC certified sites worldwide, and a large network of BRC certification bodies in 90 countries.

CASE COST REDUCTION

A type of promotion where the price of the case that's sold to the retailer is reduced.

CASE SIZE

The number of individual selling units within the outer case.

CHEP PALLET

Flat wooden delivery unit for stacking cases on. An industry standard one is 1200 x 1000mm. Most retailers when you complete the listing forms stipulate deliveries on CHEP pallets.

CLIP STRIPS

The plastic strips which hang on retailer shelves with things like crisps/nuts etc. on them. If your product can be displayed/sold from these you have more flexibility on where you can sit in store and use less shelf space.

COMMODITY CODE

The descriptive categories that items are placed into for export purposes.

CONSOLIDATION

When two or more suppliers' deliveries are grouped together on a single vehicle, reducing the number of vehicles used.

CO-PACKING
When another company packs your products to your specification using their own equipment and workforce.

COSHH
Control of Substances Hazardous to Health

CUTTER GUIDE
The technical drawing of your packaging; it is the structural framework into which your design is positioned.

DUMP BIN
Piece of fixturisation used to display items.

EAN
International Article Number (previously European Article Number); the 13 digit barcode number for an individual consumer unit.

EDI
Electronic Data Interchange, when order or invoice information is sent electronically between a supplier and retailer's systems. All the larger retailers require you to have this.

EHO
Environmental Health Officer

EPOS
Electronic Point of Sale, the method of recording a store's till sales data by scanning the product barcodes.

EXCLUSIVITY

Giving a retailer an exclusive supply of your product for a limited time. This could be just one or two from your range for say six months. It's a useful negotiation tool.

FACING

Number of units of a given SKU on the front row of the fixture.

FIFO

First In, First Out: a stock management process where the oldest product (so stock with the shortest shelf life) is dispatched before the newer stock (with a longer shelf life), so reducing inventory losses.

FTL

Full Truck Load

GONDOLA END

The selling space that is located at the end of a store aisle. They are often used for promotional or new products due to the greater consumer footfall at that location. To sit here usually means substantial investment from the brand.

GSCOP

Grocery Service Code of Practice

GTIN

Global Trade Item Number, the 14-digit outer case barcode number for the traded item.

HACCP

Hazard Analysis Critical Control Point

INCREMENTAL SALES
The increase in product sales that happens directly because of promotional or marketing activity.

JBP
Joint business plan. This is what you work out with the retailer. An agreed plan covering business objectives (sales, profit, volumes etc).

KPI
Key Performance Indicator, a performance monitoring measure of a process or company.

LEAD TIME
The amount of time between placing an order and receiving the stock. Usually the number of days.

LSP
Logistics Service Provider, a distribution company who store stock and deliver the orders to the retailers.

MARGIN
Difference between cost and retail prices.

MARGIN MAINTAINED
When your product is on promotion with a retailer, but they want margin maintained i.e. your normal RSP is £1.99 but you are on promotion at £1.49. The retailer still expects the same margin, and you as the producer take the hit on your margin.

MOQ
Minimum Order Quantity, an agreement on the smallest amount of stock that can be ordered for a single order.

NPD
New Product Development

OCADO OLIVE
Ocado's supplier portal showing product details and purchase orders. When you secure a listing with Ocado this is the system you will use for orders and invoicing.

OPEN BOOK COSTING
When all the costs for a process are visible between the service provider and customer. This includes visibility of the service provider's fee for managing the process.

OSA
On-Shelf Availability, product availability on a retailer's selling shelf.

OUT OF STOCK
When there is no stock available to fulfil a customer order.

PICKING
The activity where an individual retailer order is assembled by selecting (or 'picking') the different elements within the warehouse, case by case and product by product.

POS
Point of Sale, both the physical location itself, and the communication material that appears, where a product is displayed for sale.

PRIMARY PACKAGING
The packaging that is still with the product unit at the point of consumption.

PRINTING PLATES

These are what your printer will use to produce the packaging. They are originated from the packaging designs you provide.

PROOF

A printed sample of work to be checked for errors in text, positioning or quality of colour reproduction. Once you approve the proof, you are responsible if there are any errors.

RANGING

Term used when a new product is listed to define which stores will stock the item. When the retailers have a range review, they are looking at their range to see if they will delist any brands or increase their range.

REEFER

A refrigerated container which is used to transport chilled or frozen goods.

RESIDUAL STOCK

Stock remaining after the end of a promotion/event.

ROLL CAGE

The metal cages on wheels that can often be seen in supermarket aisles and are used to store orders, from picking in distribution centres to delivery in store.

RRP

Recommended Retail Price

RSP

Recommended Sale Price

SALSA

Safe and Legal Supplier Approval. SALSA is a food safety standard written by experienced food safety experts to reflect both the legal requirements of producers and the enhanced expectations of 'best practice' of professional food buyers.

SKU

Stock Keeping Unit: a particular product, at a set size. For instance, with Scrubbys, the four vegetable mix was available in both 40g and 100g bags. Each had their own unique SKU (pronounced skew).

SRP

Shelf Ready Packaging: when the product is in packaging that allows it to go directly onto the shelf in one touch. Retailers will talk about how many units you have in an SRP.

TOOLING CHARGE

The cost charged for creating the piece of metal equipment (known as the die) that will be used to cut out your packaging design footprint.

TOUCHPOINT

Sainsbury's supplier portal showing data including sales, depot stock and product availability.

TRADE CODE

The descriptive categories that items are placed into for export purposes.

TRIGGER FUNDING

A type of promotion funding which is linked to the redemption-rate in multibuy promotions. So it is based on till sales, triggered when people buy into the multibuy, and funded retrospectively.

TRUNKING
The transportation of product between distribution centres.

TUC
Traded Unit Code, the 14-digit barcode number on a case of product.

USP
Unique selling point

WAITROSE CONNECT
Waitrose supplier portal showing product details and purchase orders.

WHITE LABEL
When a manufacturer makes a product under your brand/label.

WOW
Week on Week

WTD
Week to Date

YOY
Year on Year

YTD
Year to Date

YTG
Year to Go

Handy reference sites for the food entrepreneur

To register your company (in the uk)

https://www.gov.uk/government/organisations/
   companies-house

For trademarking

https://www.gov.uk/government/organisations/
   intellectual-property-office

For legal and technical stuff

www.gov.uk/government/publications/
   groceries-supply-code-of-practice
www.campdenbri.co.uk
www.brandbank.com
www.brcglobalstandards.com
www.salsafood.co.uk

For barcoding

www.gs1uk.org

For research

www.bl.uk/business-and-ip-centre
www.thegrocer.co.uk
www.mintel.co.uk
www.vypr.it
www.food.gov.uk
www.iriworldwide.com
www.fdin.org.uk
www.just-food.com
www.nielsen.com

For funding

(in addition to those referred to in Chapter 6)

www.gapcap.co.uk
www.kickstarter.com
www.startuploans.co.uk
www.virginstartup.org
www.primestox.com
www.jamjarinvestments.co.uk
www.piper.co.uk

Support networks

www.facebook.com/groups/
    clairebrumbytheentrepreneurcoach/
www.facebook.com/groups/thefoodhubforum
www.foodanddrinkforum.co.uk
www.breadandjamfest.com

Trade shows

www.specialityandfinefoodfairs.co.uk
www.ife.co.uk
www.farmshopanddelishow.co.uk
www.befitlondon.com
www.naturalproducts.co.uk
www.gff.co.uk/shows/ffsn/
www.foodmatterslive.com
www.lunchshow.co.uk/
www.naturalproducts.co.uk/

Food fairs

www.foodiesfestival.com
www.bbcgoodfoodshow.com
www.gff.co.uk/shows/great-taste-markets/
www.foodfestivalfinder.co.uk

Some awards to enter

www.freefromfoodawards.co.uk
www.foodbev.com/awards
www.qualityfoodawards.com
www.greattasteawards.co.uk
www.foodmatterslive.com/get-involved/awards
www.thegrocernewproductawards.co.uk
https://nourishawards.org/

Some amazing people to know

www.janemilton.com
http://tessastuart.co.uk/
www.bradburton.biz
www.croz.uk.com
https://theeir.co/ (Will King)
www.rollits.com (Julian Wild)

Some extra 'free' bits for you, my gift so you can create your winning mix

To download the worksheets from the book, go here:
www.clairebrumby.com/your-winning-mix/

For kick-ass guerrilla marketing top tips, go here:
www.clairebrumby.com/kick-ass-stuff/

For My Winning Mix Blueprint: 44 Tips to save you time, money and sanity in your business, go here:
clairebrumby.lpages.co/my-winning-mix-blueprint/

About the Author

Claire Brumby is a coach, mentor, speaker and consultant who works with businesses nationally and internationally, from pre-start up stage to very established ones looking for growth.

She is an experienced and in demand inspirational and motivational speaker. Some additional topics include: Business, Retail, Women in Business, Embracing Change, Working Outside Your Comfort Zone, Starting a Business with No Knowledge/Experience in the Sector, Success and Failure, Mind over Matter, Launching and Building a Brand, Guerrilla Marketing, and much more.

She is also a proud mum to her 3 children, a Virgin StartUp Mentor, regular contributor to various industry blogs, a judge for The Quality Food Awards, The Great Taste Awards and The Nourish Awards, and writes and delivers seminars, workshops and masterclasses for clients including Nottingham Trent University and London Metropolitan University on subjects including: building a brand, launching a food business, routes to market, innovation, pitching to buyers and much more. Claire has appeared on national TV and been a guest on radio stations sharing her business insights.

Her kids are now 20, 17 and 14 years old, and have been through every step of this journey too; that's her reason for dedicating this book to them.

When she's not doing any of the above you'll find her in some open water somewhere, taking on swims such as Lake Coniston, Lake Windermere or the English Channel – all in all living well outside of any comfort zone and welcoming her next challenge!

Lightning Source UK Ltd.
Milton Keynes UK
UKHW020513130919
349657UK00011B/584/P